GLOBE EDUCAT
SHORTER SHAKESPEARE

ROMEO AND JULIET

- Get straight to the heart of the play
- Understand the whole story
- Read Shakespeare's language with confidence

HODDER
EDUCATION
AN HACHETTE UK COMPANY

Introduction

Shakespeare the writer

Shakespeare would probably be amazed that you are studying one of his plays in school over 400 years after his death. He did not write his plays to be read, he wrote them to be performed. When he wrote, he expected a company of skilful actors to interpret and perform his play for an audience to listen to and watch. *Romeo and Juliet* was printed in his lifetime, but eighteen of his plays were only printed after his death in a collection of his plays known as the *First Folio*.

Prose and verse

Most of the time, Shakespeare wrote *blank verse* – verse where the ends of the lines do not rhyme. So what makes it verse? It has a rhythm. Normally there are ten syllables in every line. Shakespeare wrote the lines to be spoken with the stress on every second syllable. Try saying,
"*baa-**boom** baa-**boom** baa-**boom** baa-**boom** baa-**boom***".

Moving on to a line from *Romeo and Juliet*, try saying it with the same rhythm and stress:

'*What **drawn** – and **talk** – of **peace** – I **hate** – the **word**'.

Shakespeare can break the rules of blank verse, but he does not often do so in *Romeo and Juliet*. He does use prose instead of verse. Less socially important characters often speak in prose, as do comic characters. So the Nurse and Peter speak in prose (for example, in Act 1 Scene 2). Romeo and Juliet speak to each other mainly in verse (for example, Act 1 Scene 5) while Romeo talks to Peter and the Nurse in prose (Act 2 Scene 4).

Shared lines: Sometimes Shakespeare had two characters share the ten syllables that make a line (as Capulet and Lady Capulet do on the right). He did this when he wanted the actors to keep the rhythm going. This was often to show the characters are particularly close, or when one is impatient.

Capulet	Thank me no thankings, nor, proud me no prouds,	**105**
	But fettle your fine joints 'gainst Thursday next,	
	To go with Paris to Saint Peter's Church,	
	Or I will drag thee on a hurdle thither.	
	Out you green-sickness carrion, out you baggage,	
	You tallow-face!	
Lady Capulet	Fie, fie, what, are you mad?	**110**

Counting lines: You can see the number 110 at the end of the last line on the right. It is normal to print the line number every five lines in a Shakespeare play. This helps people find an exact place when talking or writing about the play. If you count, however, you will see that line 110 is six lines from the line 105 – the two lines that make the shared line only count as one.

How to use this book

Act and Scene: Printed plays are divided into Acts and Scenes. On the stage there is no real gap – a new scene happens when the story moves on, either to a new time or place. When Shakespeare's company performed indoors by candlelight they needed to trim the candles about every half an hour, so they picked points in the story where a short gap between scenes made sense. These became the divisions between Acts.

Elision: Elision is the correct term in English Literature for leaving a bit out. Shakespeare does it a lot. Often he can not quite fit what he wants to say into his ten-syllable line, so he cheats – running two words together. In the highlighted example, do not say *stolen*, pronouncing the *-en* at the end, but say *stoln*, running the *l* and *n* together. The inverted comma shows you there is something missing.

Act 2 Scene 1

Enter Romeo alone.

Romeo	Can I go forward when my heart is here? Turn back, dull earth, and find thy centre out.
	Enter Benvolio with Mercutio. Romeo hides.
Benvolio	Romeo! My cousin Romeo! Romeo!
Mercutio	On my life hath stol'n him home to bed.

Stage Directions: Shakespeare wrote stage directions – mainly when characters enter or exit, but sometimes telling actors what to do. In this book we develop Shakespeare's stage directions a bit, to tell you what you would see if you were watching the play.

Some stage directions are in square brackets, we print them as part of an actor's lines. These help you understand who the actor is talking to – which would be obvious on stage. *Aside* is a significant one – this is when the character shares their thoughts with the audience.

Romeo	*[To a Servingman.]* What lady is that which doth enrich the hand Of yonder knight? *[Aside.]* O, she doth teach the torches to burn bright! **5** It seems she hangs upon the cheek of night

7 **Ethiope:** a black African (from Ethiopia)

8 **Beauty too rich ... too dear:** too beautiful to live an ordinary life on

The glossary: Some words and phrases have changed their meaning or fallen out of use since Shakespeare's time. The glossary helps you with them. It gives you the line numbers in the play (in red); then the word, or the start and end of a long phrase (with three dots to mark the elision where some words have been left out), in **bold**; then the explanation in modern English. It is as close to the original line as we can make it.

Romeo (left) and Benvolio (right).
Where might Benvolio have put his blazer back on?

The questions: There are questions in the photograph captions, and in red boxes. Here are two tips for answering them:

- There usually is not a simple 'right' answer. We hope you will develop your own ideas. The best way to answer any question is to be able to back up your answer with a reference to the play text.

- Unless we tell you otherwise, you can answer the question using the play text on the opposite page.

The Globe Theatre

Today's *Shakespeare's Globe* in London was built to show us what open-air theatres were like in Shakespeare's time. It is very different from other modern theatres. Shakespeare wrote *Romeo and Juliet* for a theatre very like the modern Globe – so how was the play affected by the theatre it was written for?

- **The stage** was large, and stuck out into the audience, who surround it on three sides. The theatre was open-air, but a roof over the stage, called the *Heavens*, kept the actors (and their expensive costumes) dry if it rained. Two large pillars held up this roof, and the actors had to move around them.

- **The upper stage** was a balcony running along the back wall of the stage. Actors and musicians could use it. Also, it was the most expensive place for members of the audience to sit (people who sat there could seen by the rest of the audience in their fine clothes).

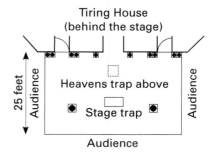

The stage trap opened into the area under the stage. The heavens trap was not on the stage, but above it. Actors playing gods might be lowered down to the stage through it.

Sam Wanamaker, an American actor and director, founded the Shakespeare's Globe Trust in 1970. Sam could not understand why there was not a proper memorial to the world's greatest playwright in the city where he had lived and worked. He started fundraising to build a new Globe Theatre. Sadly, Sam died before the theatre opened in 1997.

- **The entrances** were in the back wall of the stage, leading from the *Tiring House* (the actors' dressing room). There was a big door in the middle and a smaller door on either side. The big entrance was useful for bringing on large props like a bed, needed for Act 4 Scene 3.

- **Traps** allowed props or actors to appear or disappear from the Heavens or into the stage. The stage trap opened into the area under the stage. The Heavens trap was not on the stage, but above it, in the Heavens.

- **The audience** The theatre held well over 2,000 people (today's Globe holds 1,700). All the audience were close to the stage. People could pay a penny to stand in the open air in the Yard around the stage. Three tiers of roofed Galleries surrounded the Yard, where, for more money, people could sit on benches.

- **Sound, light and scenery** – there was not any, except for daylight, live music, and live sound effects (like rolling a cannonball in a trough to make a sound like thunder). The Globe was not dark, like a modern theatre; the actors and audience could all see each other – all the time. Shakespeare often started a play with a dramatic and noisy moment to grab the audience's attention. Characters often describe where they are, or that it was dark – see lines 13–15 of Act 2 Scene 1 (page 29).

The full text of part of Act 1 Scene 1 (lines 99–124), showing the cuts in the *Shorter Shakespeare* text.

Benvolio	Here were the servants of your adversary, And yours, close fighting ere I did approach.	100
	I drew to part them. In the instant came The fiery Tybalt, with his sword prepared, Which, as he breathed defiance to my ears, He swung about his head and cut the winds, Who nothing hurt withal, hissed him in scorn.	105
	While we were interchanging thrusts and blows, Came more and more, and fought on part and part, Till the Prince came, who parted either part.	
Lady Montague	O, where is Romeo, saw you him to-day? Right glad I am he was not at this fray.	110
Benvolio	Madam, an hour before the worshipped sun Peered forth the golden window of the east, A troubled mind drove me to walk abroad, Where, underneath the grove of sycamore That westward rooteth from the city side,	115
	So early walking did I see your son. Towards him I made, but he was ware of me And stole into the covert of the wood. I, measuring his affections by my own, Which then most sought where most might not be found,	120
	Being one too many by my weary self, That most are busied when they're most alone, Pursued my humour not pursuing his, And gladly shunned who gladly fled from me.	

What is 'Shorter Shakespeare'?

In the texts that survive, Shakespeare's plays are of very different lengths. The longest is 3,904 lines, and the shortest 1,918 lines (*Romeo and Juliet* is 3,185 lines). Plays were said to take about two hours in Shakespeare's time (3,900 lines would take about 4 hours), so his company must have *cut* the play for performance. This could have meant leaving out whole scenes, and/ or shortening speeches throughout the play. Almost all productions of Shakespeare's plays ever since have made some cuts to the text.

Shorter Shakespeare cuts the play to help you study it in the classroom. Our cut is about 1,560 lines, and we have 'filleted' the text, so you get all the important parts. We do not add to, or change, the words – Shakespeare originally wrote them all. The example on the left shows you the sort of things we have cut (from Act 1 Scene 1).

The Prologue

Enter Chorus.

Chorus   Two households, both alike in dignity,
(In fair Verona, where we lay our scene),
From ancient grudge break to new mutiny,
Where civil blood makes civil hands unclean.
From forth the fatal loins of these two foes   5
A pair of star-crossed lovers take their life,
Whose misadventured piteous overthrows
Doth with their death bury their parents' strife.
The fearful passage of their death-marked love,
And the continuance of their parents' rage   10
(Which but their children's end, nought could remove),
Is now the two hours' traffic of our stage.
The which if you with patient ears attend,
What here shall miss, our toil shall strive to mend.

Exit.

1 **dignity:** social status
3 **ancient grudge:** old quarrels
3 **break to new mutiny:** begin new quarrels
4 **Where civil blood ... hands unclean:** fighting and spilling blood even though they are not soldiers at war
5 **From forth the fatal loins ... two foes:** from these two warring households
6 **star-crossed:** doomed by fate
7 **misadventured piteous overthows:** tragic, steps to ruin
12 **traffic of our stage:** subject of our play
14 **What here shall miss ... to mend:** We'll work hard to tell you the full story

Tybalt (right) fighting Benvolio (left) in the opening scene.
What impression does the director's choice of clothes and the age of the actors give about this fight that opens the play?
What impression does this photograph give you of Tybalt?

Act 1 Scene 1

Enter Sampson and Gregory, of the house of Capulet, armed with swords and bucklers.

Sampson	A dog of the house of Montague moves me.
Gregory	To move is to stir; and to be valiant is to stand. Therefore, if thou art moved, thou runn'st away.
Sampson	A dog of that house shall move me to stand. I will take the wall of any man or maid of Montague's. Draw thy tool, here comes two of the house of the Montagues. 5

Enter Abraham and Balthasar, serving men of the Montagues.

Sampson	My naked weapon is out. Quarrel, I will back thee.
Abraham	Do you bite your thumb at us, sir?
Sampson	I do bite my thumb, sir.
Abraham	Do you bite your thumb at us, sir? 10
Sampson	*[Aside to Gregory.]* Is the law of our side, if I say 'ay'?
Gregory	*[Aside to Sampson.]* No.
Sampson	No, sir, I do not bite my thumb at you, sir. But I bite my thumb, sir.
Gregory	Do you quarrel, sir? 15
Abraham	Quarrel, sir? No, sir.
Sampson	If you do, sir, I am for you. I serve as good a man as you.
Abraham	No better?
Sampson	Well, sir –
Gregory	Say "better". 20
Sampson	Yes, better, sir.
Abraham	You lie.
Sampson	Draw if you be men. *[They fight.]*

Enter Benvolio.

Benvolio	*[Drawing his sword.]* Part, fools! Put up your swords, you know not what you do. 25

Enter Tybalt.

Tybalt	What, art thou drawn among these heartless hinds? Turn thee, Benvolio, look upon thy death.
Benvolio	I do but keep the peace.
Tybalt	What, drawn, and talk of peace? I hate the word, As I hate hell, all Montagues, and thee. 30 Have at thee, coward! *[They fight].*

Enter several Montagues and Capulets who join in the fight, also an officer and three or four citizens with clubs or partisans.

2 **stir:** run away
2 **stand:** stay and fight
4 **move:** make me angry enough to
4–5 **take the wall:** walk by the wall (the best part of the street) furthest from the centre of the street where the gutter was
6 **tool:** sword
7 **My naked weapon is out:** my sword is out of my scabbard
7 **Quarrel:** start a fight
7 **back thee:** back you up
7 **bite your thumb:** [an insulting gesture at the time[
17 **I am for you:** I'll fight you
25 **Put up:** put away
26 **heartless hinds:** cowardly servants (double meaning of female deer without a male for protection)
28 **I do but keep the peace:** I'm just trying to stop this fighting

1 When Shakespeare wrote this play, family honour was very important. It often led to fights, and sometimes deaths. How does the opening scene show the audience the role that family honour played in Verona?

Capulet (left) and Montague (right) fighting. In this production they entered from opposite sides of the Yard, and started fighting before they got onto the stage. Compare this photograph with the one on the previous page. Which is more surprising? What does this tell you about the feud between the Montagues and the Capulets?

Officer	Clubs, bills, and partisans! Strike! Beat them down! Down with the Capulets! Down with the Montagues!	
	Enter Capulet in his gown, and Lady Capulet.	
Capulet	What noise is this? Give me my long sword, ho!	
	Enter Montague and Lady Montague.	
Montague	Thou villain Capulet. — Hold me not, let me go.	35
Lady Montague	Thou shalt not stir one foot to seek a foe.	
	Enter Prince Escalus, with his Attendants.	
Prince	Rebellious subjects, enemies to peace, Profaners of this neighbour-stainèd steel, — Throw your mistempered weapons to the ground, And hear the sentence of your movèd Prince. Three civil brawls, bred of an airy word, By thee, old Capulet, and Montague, Have thrice disturbed the quiet of our streets. If ever you disturb our streets again, Your lives shall pay the forfeit of the peace. For this time on pain of death, all men depart.	40 45
	Exit all but Montague, Lady Montague, and Benvolio.	
Montague	Who set this ancient quarrel new abroach? Speak, nephew, were you by when it began?	
Benvolio	I drew to part them. In the instant came The fiery Tybalt, with his sword prepared, Which, as he breathed defiance to my ears, He swung about his head and cut the winds, Who nothing hurt withal, hissed him in scorn.	50
Lady Montague	O, where is Romeo, saw you him to-day? Right glad I am he was not at this fray.	55
Benvolio	Madam, an hour before the worshipped sun Peered forth the golden window of the east, A troubled mind drove me to walk abroad, So early walking did I see your son. Towards him I made, but he was ware of me And stole into the covert of the wood.	60
Montague	Many a morning hath he there been seen, With tears augmenting the fresh morning's dew, Adding to clouds more clouds with his deep sighs.	
Benvolio	My noble uncle, do you know the cause?	65
Montague	I neither know it, nor can learn of him.	
	Enter Romeo.	
Benvolio	See, where he comes. So please you step aside, I'll know his grievance, or be much denied.	

32 **bills, and partisans:** types of spear

34 **long sword:** old-fashioned heavy sword

38 **Profaners of this neighbour-stainèd steel:** who have shown contempt for my orders and God by fighting and wounding fellow citizens
39 **mistempered:** used with a double meaning of 'badly made' (for swords) and 'angry' for the people using them
40 **sentence:** punishment
40 **movèd:** angry
41 **civil brawls:** outbreaks of fighting between citizens
41 **bred of an airy word:** over some trivial remark
45 **Your lives ... the peace:** you'll be executed
47 **set this ... new abroach:** started this old quarrel up again
48 **by:** nearby
53 **Who nothing hurt withal:** which, unharmed
55 **Right glad ... this fray:** I'm very glad he wasn't part of this fight

60 **made:** went
60 **he was ware of me:** he noticed me
61 **covert:** shelter
63 **augmenting:** adding to

67 **So please you:** please
68 **his grievance ... denied:** what's upsetting him, I won't take no for an answer

Romeo (left) and Benvolio (right)
When might Benvolio have put his blazer back on?

These questions are about all of Act 1 Scene 1.

2 What impressions of Romeo's feelings are given by the language he uses in this scene?

3 What impression do the audience have of Romeo when he appears?

Views of romantic love in Shakespeare's time

In this scene, Romeo and Benvolio talk about love. Romeo feels that love has changed him completely: 'This is not Romeo, he's some other where.' In Shakespeare's time, romantic love was often viewed with suspicion: love was expected to grow after marriage – not sweep a couple off their feet beforehand. Marriages were often arranged by families, not by the couple to be married.

Loving someone too much was seen as an illness, a form of short-term madness. Unrequited love was often called 'lovesickness', and treated as a disease that could also send people mad. Doctors were sometimes consulted. They prescribed a variety of 'cures', from herbal medicines, to changed diets, to talking to a priest.

Montague	Come madam, let's away.

Exit Montague and Lady Montague.

Benvolio	Good morrow, cousin.	
Romeo	Is the day so young?	70
Benvolio	But new struck nine.	
Romeo	Ay me, sad hours seem long. Was that my father that went hence so fast?	
Benvolio	It was. What sadness lengthens Romeo's hours?	
Romeo	Not having that, which having, makes them short.	
Benvolio	In love?	75
Romeo	Out —	
Benvolio	Of love?	
Romeo	Out of her favour, where I am in love.	
Benvolio	Alas that love, so gentle in his view, Should be so tyrannous and rough in proof!	80
Romeo	Alas, that love, whose view is muffled still, Should without eyes see pathways to his will. — Where shall we dine? — O me! What fray was here? Yet tell me not, for I have heard it all. Here's much to do with hate, but more with love.	85
	Why, then, O brawling love, O loving hate, O any thing, of nothing first created. This love feel I, that feel no love in this. Dost thou not laugh?	
Benvolio	No, coz, I rather weep.	
Romeo	Good heart, at what?	
Benvolio	At thy good heart's oppression.	90
Romeo	Why such is love's transgression. Farewell, my coz.	
Benvolio	Soft! I will go along. And if you leave me so, you do me wrong.	
Romeo	Tut, I have lost myself, I am not here, This is not Romeo, he's some other where.	95
Benvolio	Tell me in sadness, who is that you love?	
Romeo	What, shall I groan and tell thee?	
Benvolio	Groan? Why, no. But sadly tell me who.	
Romeo	In sadness, cousin, I do love a woman.	
Benvolio	I aimed so near when I supposed you loved.	100
Romeo	A right good mark-man, and she's fair I love.	
Benvolio	A right fair mark, fair coz, is soonest hit.	
Romeo	Well, in that hit you miss, she'll not be hit	

[Handwritten annotation: unrequited love = love w/someone but they don't love you.]

[Handwritten annotation at line 85: love of family]

Glossary:

70 **morrow:** morning

70 **cousin:** used to close relatives and friends

72 **hence:** away from here

78 **Out of her favour:** no longer loved

79 **so gentle in his view:** so attractive as an idea

80 **be so …. in proof:** treat us so badly when we experience it

81 **whose view … still:** refers Cupid, the god of love, who was said to be blind or blindfolded

82 **see pathways to his will:** can still make what he wants happen

87 **of nothing first created:** made from nothing at the start

88 **This love... in this:** I love, but am not loved in return

89 **coz:** cousin

89 **rather weep:** weep instead

90 **oppression:** heaviness, misery

91 **love's transgression:** the way love steps outside its proper limits

92 **Soft!:** wait!

96 **in sadness:** in all seriousness

100 **I aimed ... you loved:** I'd worked that out when I guessed you were in love

101 **A right good mark-man:** an excellent guess

102 **A right fair mark:** an easy target

ABOVE Capulet and Paris, 16th-century costumes
Who is Capulet's social equal – Paris or Peter? Which one is of lower social status?
How many reasons can you find to support your answer?
BELOW Peter and Capulet, modern-dress production

	With Cupid's arrow. She hath Dian's wit.
	She will not stay the siege of loving terms, **105**
	Nor bide th' encounter of assailing eyes,
	Nor ope her lap to saint-seducing gold.
	O she is rich in beauty, only poor
	That when she dies, with beauty dies her store.
Benvolio	Then she hath sworn that she will still live chaste? **110**
Romeo	She hath, and in that sparing makes huge waste.
Benvolio	Be ruled by me, forget to think of her.
Romeo	O teach me how I should forget to think.
Benvolio	By giving liberty unto thine eyes,
	Examine other beauties. **115**
Romeo	Show me a mistress that is passing fair.
	What doth her beauty serve but as a note,
	Where I may read who passed that passing fair?
	Farewell, thou canst not teach me to forget.
Benvolio	I'll pay that doctrine, or else die in debt. *They exit.*

104 Dian's wit: the skills of Diana, the goddess of chastity

105–6 stay the siege... assailing eyes: listen to a lover's words or even let him gaze adoringly

107 Nor ope … gold: you can't buy her love, either

109 her store: the virginity she's been saving

111 sparing: saving, hoarding up

118 Where I may... fair: that reminds me my love is more beautiful

120 I'll pay... in debt: I will teach you that or die trying

Act 1 Scene 2

Enter Capulet, Paris and Peter.

Paris	But now, my lord, what say you to my suit?
Capulet	But saying o'er what I have said before.
	My child is yet a stranger in the world,
	She hath not seen the change of fourteen years,
	Let two more summers wither in their pride, **5**
	Ere we may think her ripe to be a bride.
Paris	Younger than she are happy mothers made.
Capulet	And too soon marred are those so early made.
	But woo her, gentle Paris, get her heart,
	My will to her consent is but a part. **10**
	And she agreed, within her scope of choice
	Lies my consent and fair according voice.
	This night I hold an old accustomed feast,
	Whereto I have invited many a guest,
	Such as I love, and you among the store, **15**
	One more, most welcome, makes my number more.
	Come, go with me. *[To Peter, giving him a paper.]*
	Go, sirrah, trudge about
	Through fair Verona, find those persons out
	Whose names are written there, and to them say,
	My house and welcome on their pleasure stay. **20**
	Exit Capulet and Paris.
Peter	I am sent to find those persons whose names are here
	writ, and can never find what names the writing person

1 suit: request

2 But: [as used here] nothing more than

3 yet … world: very young

6 Ere: before

7 Younger … mothers made: younger girls are married with children

8 too soon marred .... made: they are spoiled by it

10 My will … a part: she has to agree as well

11–2 And she... according voice: I'll accept any suitable person she chooses

13 old accustomed: traditional

14 Whereto: to which

15 the store: them

17 sirrah: you [used to a less important person]

20 stay: wait

22–3 can never ... here writ: can't read

13

These questions are about all of Act 1 Scene 2.

1 What imagery used by Romeo in this scene shows the audience that he thinks Rosaline is superior to any other possible lover?

2 How is Benvolio's character shown in this scene?

3 How would you tell the actor playing Benvolio to move and speak as he tries to persuade Romeo to give up his love for Rosaline?

4 Power and wealth are important in the play. How does this scene show the audience the importance of wealth and power?

Benvolio and Romeo
Which line do you think was being spoken when this photograph was taken – line 25, line 45, or line 55?

hath here writ. I must to the learnèd. — In good time.

Enter Benvolio and Romeo, talking.

Benvolio	Why, Romeo, art thou mad?	
Romeo	Not mad, but bound more than a mad-man is:	25
	Shut up in prison, kept without my food,	
	Whipped and tormented and — Good e'en, good fellow.	
Peter	God gi' good e'en. I pray, sir, can you read?	
Romeo	Ay, if I know the letters and the language.	
Peter	Ye say honestly, rest you merry!	30
Romeo	Stay, fellow; I can read. *[He reads the list.]*	
	Signior Martino and his wife and daughters; County	
	Anselme and his beauteous sisters; the lady widow of	
	Vitruvio; Signior Placentio and his lovely nieces;	
	Mercutio and his brother Valentine; mine uncle	35
	Capulet, his wife and daughters; my fair niece	
	Rosaline; Livia; Signior Valentio and his cousin	
	Tybalt; Lucio and the lively Helena.	
	A fair assembly: whither should they come?	
Peter	Up.	40
Romeo	Whither? To supper?	
Peter	To our house.	
Romeo	Whose house?	
Peter	My master's.	
Romeo	Indeed I should have asked you that before.	45
Peter	Now I'll tell you without asking. My master is the	
	great rich Capulet, and if you be not of the house of	
	Montagues, I pray, come and crush a cup of wine.	
	Rest you merry! *He exits.*	
Benvolio	At this same ancient feast of Capulet's	50
	Sups the fair Rosaline, whom thou so loves,	
	With all the admired beauties of Verona.	
	Go thither and with unattainted eye,	
	Compare her face with some that I shall show,	
	And I will make thee think thy swan a crow.	55
Romeo	One fairer than my love? The all-seeing sun	
	Ne'er saw her match since first the world begun.	
Benvolio	Tut, you saw her fair, none else being by,	
	But in that crystal scales let there be weighed	
	Your lady's love against some other maid	60
	That I will show you shining at this feast,	
	And she shall scant show well that now seems best.	
Romeo	I'll go along, no such sight to be shown,	
	But to rejoice in splendour of mine own. *Exit both.*	

27 Good-e'en: a greeting used after midday

28 gi': give you

30 rest you merry: farewell

32 County: Count

39 whither … come?: where are they invited?

48 crush: drink

51 Sups: has her supper

53 thither: there

53 unattainted: unprejudiced

58 none else being by: with no other beauties nearby

59 that crystal scales: your eyes

60 Your lady's love: the love you have for Rosaline

62 she shall scant … seems best: and the one you love best now will not seem anywhere near as beautiful

64 splendour of mine own: in how much more beautiful my love is than the rest

A

The Nurse and Juliet

One of these photographs was taken around lines 24–5 and the other around line 41. Which is which?

B

Juliet and her Nurse

In Shakespeare's time. most families that could afford it had a nurse to bring up their children. A family like the Capulets certainly would. These children saw very little of their parents. Nurses were servants, but they were more important than servants who cooked and cleaned. The Nurse in *Romeo and Juliet* has brought Juliet up from a baby. She breast-fed her, took care of her during the day and slept in her room at night. Juliet spent far more time with the Nurse than with anyone else, and Shakespeare suggests she is closer to the Nurse than to her mother.

Act 1 Scene 3

Enter Lady Capulet and Nurse.

Lady Capulet	Nurse, where's my daughter? Call her forth to me.
Nurse	Now, by my maidenhead at twelve year old I bade her come. What, lamb! What, ladybird! God forbid, where's this girl? What, Juliet!

Enter Juliet.

Juliet	How now, who calls?	**5**
Nurse	Your mother.	
Juliet	Madam, I am here. What is your will?	
Lady Capulet	This is the matter. — Nurse, give leave awhile, We must talk in secret. — Nurse, come back again, I have remembered me, thou's hear our counsel. Thou knowest my daughter's of a pretty age.	**10**
Nurse	Faith, I can tell her age unto an hour.	
Lady Capulet	She's not fourteen.	
Nurse	I'll lay fourteen of my teeth (and yet I have but four), she's not fourteen. How long is it now to Lammas-tide?	
Lady Capulet	A fortnight and odd days.	**16**
Nurse	Even or odd, of all days in the year, come Lammas-eve at night shall she be fourteen. Susan and she (God rest all Christian souls) were of an age. Well, Susan is with God, she was too good for me. But, as I said, on Lammas Eve at night shall she be fourteen. 'Tis since the earthquake now eleven years, and she was weaned (I never shall forget it) of all the days of the year, upon that day, for she could have run and waddled all about. For even the day before, she broke her brow: and then my husband (God be with his soul, a' was a merry man) took up the child, "Yea", quoth he, "dost thou fall upon thy face? Thou wilt fall backward when thou hast more wit, Wilt thou not, Jule?" And, by my holidam, the pretty wretch left crying and said "Ay".	**20** **25** **30**
Lady Capulet	Enough of this, I pray thee, hold thy peace.	
Nurse	Yes, madam, yet I cannot choose but laugh, To think it should leave crying and say "Ay". And yet, I warrant, it had upon its brow A bump as big as a young cockerel's stone. A perilous knock, and it cried bitterly. "Yea", quoth my husband, "fall'st upon thy face? Thou wilt fall backward when thou comest to age, Wilt thou not, Jule?" It stinted and said "Ay".	**35**
Juliet	And stint thou too, I pray thee nurse, say I.	**40**

2 **maidenhead:** virginity
3 **bade:** told her to

7 **What is your will?:** what can I do for you?
8 **the matter:** what I want to discuss
8 **give leave:** leave us
10 **thou's hear our counsel:** you shall hear our discussion
11 **pretty age:** suitable age for marriage

14 **but:** only
15 **Lammas-tide:** a holy day, 1 August

18 **Susan:** the Nurse's daughter
19 **of an age:** the same age

22 **was weaned:** stopped breastfeeding

25 **broke her brow:** cut her forehead
26 **a':** he
28 **Thou wilt fall backward:** sexual double meaning
28–9 **thou hast more wit:** you're wiser
29 **by my holidam:** by my holy lady (a way of swearing you are telling the truth)
30 **left:** stopped
31 **hold thy peace:** that's enough talking
33 **it:** the baby, Juliet
35 **stone:** testicle
38 **comest to age:** are old enough
39 **stinted:** stopped crying

The Nurse helping to dress Juliet
Compare this photograph with the ones on page 16.
How far do they show a similar relationship?

These questions are about all of Act 1 Scene 3.

1 How does the way in which the Nurse speaks
   show the audience what she is like?

2 How is the position of women and girls introduced
   in this scene?

Arranged marriages

In Shakespeare's time, marriages, especially in important families, were usually arranged by the couple's families.
However, this was beginning to shift towards marriages based on the attraction between the two people to be married.
Arranged marriages were usually based on the wealth and importance of the families involved. Parents (usually fathers)
tried to find a suitable husband for their daughters – someone from a family at least as wealthy and important as their own.

Women usually married in their mid-twenties, and men in their late twenties. The children of the wealthy often married
younger than this; but not as young as Juliet.

Nurse	Peace, I have done. God mark thee to his grace,
	Thou wast the prettiest babe that e'er I nursed.
	And I might live to see thee married once,
	I have my wish.
Lady Capulet	Marry, that "marry" is the very theme 45
	I came to talk of. Tell me, daughter Juliet,
	How stands your disposition to be married?
Juliet	It is an honour that I dream not of.
Lady Capulet	Well, think of marriage now. Younger than you
	Here in Verona, ladies of esteem,
	Are made already mothers. By my count 50
	I was your mother much upon these years
	That you are now a maid. Thus then in brief:
	The valiant Paris seeks you for his love.
Nurse	A man, young lady. Lady, such a man. 55
Lady Capulet	Verona's summer hath not such a flower.
Nurse	Nay he's a flower, in faith a very flower.
Lady Capulet	What say you, can you love the gentleman?
	This night you shall behold him at our feast.
	Read o'er the volume of young Paris' face, 60
	And find delight writ there with beauty's pen.
	This precious book of love, this unbound lover,
	To beautify him, only lacks a cover.
	Speak briefly, can you like of Paris' love?
Juliet	I'll look to like, if looking liking move. 65
	But no more deep will I endart mine eye
	Than your consent gives strength to make it fly.

Enter Servant.

Peter	Madam, the guests are come, supper served up, you
	called, my young lady asked for, the nurse cursed in the
	pantry, and everything in extremity. I must hence to 70
	wait. I beseech you follow straight. *He exits.*
Lady Capulet	We follow thee. Juliet, the County stays.
Nurse	Go, girl, seek happy nights to happy days. *They exit.*

Act 1 Scene 4

Enter torch-bearers, Romeo, Mercutio, Benvolio, with five or six friends as masquers.

Romeo	Give me a torch, I am not for this ambling.
	Being but heavy I will bear the light.
Mercutio	Nay, gentle Romeo, we must have you dance.
Romeo	Not I, believe me. You have dancing shoes
	With nimble soles, I have a soul of lead 5

43 And I might: if I could just

43 once: one day

45 Marry: a mild oath – by Mary (Christ's mother)

47 How stands your disposition: how do you feel about …

50 ladies of esteem: well-respected women of good social status

52–3 much upon these years … now a maid: at about your age

59 behold: see

60 Read o'er … Paris' face: Lady Capulet uses a book metaphor throughout this speech; Juliet has to 'read' Paris' potential as a husband

62 unbound: double meaning: incomplete because unmarried; a book with no cover

63 To beautify … a cover: needs a wife to be complete

64 like of: accept

65 I'll look … liking move: I'll go hoping to like him

66–7 no more deep … make it fly: I won't like him any more than you think I should

70 in extremity: needs doing at once

70 to wait: to serve the food and drink

71 straight: straight away

72 the County stays: the Count is waiting

Stage direction masquers: masked entertainers

1 I am … ambling: I don't want to dance

2 heavy: sad

Benvolio, Romeo and Mercutio in fancy dress, on their way to gatecrash the Capulets' party. (This is from a modern-dress production.)
What part of the Batman and Robin costumes have they not yet put on? How will this help them gatecrash the party?

Masques and masks

In Shakespeare's time, royal and noble families hired musicians and actors to entertain their guests at grand celebrations in their own houses. At some of these events, a masque might be performed.

A masque could be a full-scale theatrical performance. Actors, and sometimes guests, sang, acted and danced in costumes and masks, with sound effects and props. These masques were expensive to produce, and were most often performed at the royal court. Women could take part because the performance was not in public. Noble families held simpler masques. They also held masques that were parties (with food, drink and dancing), where the guests wore fancy-dress and masks.

The Capulets' party in *Romeo and Juliet* did not have theatrical performances, but there was eating, drinking and dancing. Romeo and his friends were able to gatecrash the party because people went in disguise. There was a tradition that a group of masked people, usually young men, could gatecrash a party such as this, as long as they behaved themselves.

	So stakes me to the ground I cannot move.	
Mercutio	You are a lover; borrow Cupid's wings And soar with them above a common bound.	
Romeo	I am too sore enpiercèd with his shaft To soar with his light feathers, and so bound Under love's heavy burden do I sink.	10
Mercutio	And, to sink in it, should you burden love, Romeo Too great oppression for a tender thing.	
Romeo	Is love a tender thing? It is too rough, Too rude, too boisterous, and it pricks like thorn.	15
Mercutio	If love be rough with you, be rough with love, Prick love for pricking, and you beat love down.	
Benvolio	Come, knock and enter; and no sooner in, But every man betake him to his legs.	
Romeo	And we mean well in going to this masque, But 'tis no wit to go.	20
Mercutio	Why, may one ask?	
Romeo	I dreamt a dream to-night.	
Mercutio	And so did I.	
Romeo	Well, what was yours?	
Mercutio	That dreamers often lie.	
Romeo	In bed asleep, while they do dream things true.	
Mercutio	O, then, I see Queen Mab hath been with you. She is the fairies' midwife, and she comes In shape no bigger than an agate-stone On the fore-finger of an alderman, Drawn with a team of little atomies Over men's noses as they lie asleep. Her chariot is an empty hazel-nut, Her wagon-spokes made of long spinners' legs, Her whip of cricket's bone, the lash of film, Her wagoner a small grey-coated gnat, Not so big as a round little worm Pricked from the lazy finger of a maid; And in this state she gallops night by night: Through lovers' brains, and then they dream of love; O'er ladies' lips, who straight on kisses dream; Which oft the angry Mab with blisters plagues, Because their breaths with sweetmeats tainted are. Sometime she driveth o'er a soldier's neck, And then dreams he of cutting foreign throats. This is the hag, when maids lie on their backs, That presses them and learns them first to bear, Making them women of good carriage.	25 30 35 40 45

6 **So stakes me:** that so fixes me

8 **common bound:** normal limit

9 **sore … his shaft:** deeply in love, pierced by Cupid's arrow

10 **and so bound:** and held back like this

11–2 **to sink… tender thing:** be careful not to put too great a burden on something as easily damaged as love

17 **Prick love … beat love down:** act on your feelings and you will control love, not be controlled by it

19 **betake him to his legs:** start dancing

21 **'tis no wit to go:** it isn't wise to go

24 **while:** sometimes

25 **Queen Mab:** a powerful fairy

26 **fairies' midwife:** the fairy who delivers dreams to humans

27 **agate-stone:** agate was used to make rings carved with tiny pictures

28 **alderman:** an important town councillor

29 **atomies:** tiny creatures

32 **spinners:** spiders

33 **film:** very, very thin threads

34 **wagoner:** driver

37 **state:** magnificence

40 **oft:** often

41 **sweetmeats:** sweet food

41 **tainted:** spoiled

45 **bear:** carry the weight of a man during sex or a baby in pregnancy. This is the start of a series of sexual double meanings

46 **of good carriage:** able to bear these weights

Asides

Asides are lines a character speaks to the audience that most, or all, of the other people on stage cannot hear. Shakespeare uses them to show the audience what the character really thinks or feels. Romeo's aside (Act 1 Scene 5, lines 4–9) tells the audience the effect that seeing Juliet has had on him. Mercutio also reveals his, very different, feelings (lines 10–5).

These questions refer to all of Act 1 Scene 4.

1 How do the words and imagery Romeo uses in this scene show the audience that he is unhappy?

2 How is the theme of dreams and the supernatural developed in this scene?

3 What impression is formed of Mercutio in this scene?

Tybalt (far left) spots Romeo (far right). Juliet is dancing with a masked man behind Romeo.
Do you think Romeo is speaking lines 3–4 or 5–10 when this photograph was taken?

This is she —

Romeo   Peace, peace, Mercutio, peace,
Thou talk'st of nothing.

Mercutio   True, I talk of dreams,
Which are the children of an idle brain,
And more inconstant than the wind, who woos   50
Even now the frozen bosom of the north.

Benvolio   This wind, you talk of blows us from ourselves,
Supper is done, and we shall come too late.

Romeo   I fear, too early, for my mind misgives,
Some consequence yet hanging in the stars   55
Shall bitterly begin his fearful date
With this night's revels, and expire the term
Of a despisèd life closed in my breast
By some vile forfeit of untimely death.
But he that hath the steerage of my course,   60
Direct my sail. On, lusty gentlemen.

Benvolio   Strike drum.

They march about the stage, and stand to one side.

48 nothing: a double meaning: nothing; 'no-thing', a slang reference to the vagina at the time
52 blows us from ourselves: distracts us
54 my mind misgives: I have a bad feeling about this
55 yet ... the stars: fated to happen in the future
56–7 Shall bitterly ... night's revels: will be set in motion at this party
57–9 and expire... untimely death: ending with my death
60 he that hath ... my course: God, who guides my life

Act 1 Scene 5

Enter Capulet, Capulet's cousin, Lady Capulet, Juliet, Tybalt, and all the guests at one door, and Romeo and the masquers at another door.

Capulet   Welcome, gentlemen, and foot it, girls.

Music plays and they dance.

Romeo   *[To a Servingman.]*
What lady is that which doth enrich the hand
Of yonder knight?
[Aside.] O, she doth teach the torches to burn bright!
It seems she hangs upon the cheek of night   5
As a rich jewel in an Ethiope's ear.
Beauty too rich for use, for earth too dear.
Did my heart love till now? Forswear it sight,
For I ne'er saw true beauty till this night.

Tybalt   *[Aside.]* This, by his voice, should be a Montague.   10
What, dares the slave
Come hither covered with an antic face,
To fleer and scorn at our solemnity?
Now, by the stock and honour of my kin,
To strike him dead I hold it not a sin.   15

Capulet   Why, how now, kinsman, wherefore storm you so?

Tybalt   Uncle, this is a Montague, our foe

6 Ethiope: a black African (from Ethiopia)
7 Beauty too rich ... too dear: too beautiful to live an ordinary life on Earth
8 Forswear it sight: deny it, my eyes
11 slave: used as an insult
12 hither: here
12 antic face: mask
13 fleer and ... solemnity: mock our celebration
14 the stock ... of my kin: my family's honour
16 wherefore storm you so?: why are you so angry?

23

	A villain that is hither come in spite,		
	To scorn at our solemnity this night.		
Capulet	Young Romeo is it?	**20**	
Tybalt	'Tis he, that villain Romeo.		
Capulet	Content thee, gentle coz, let him alone,		
	'A bears him like a portly gentleman,		
	Therefore be patient, take no note of him.		
Tybalt	It fits, when such a villain is a guest.	**25**	
	I'll not endure him.		
Capulet	He shall be endured.		
	What, goodman boy! I say he shall! Go to!		
	Am I the master here or you? Go to!		
Tybalt	Why, uncle, 'tis a shame.		
Capulet	Go to, go to!		
	You are a saucy boy. Is't so indeed? —	**30**	
	Well said, my hearts. — You are a princox, go, —		
	I'll make you quiet. — What, cheerly my hearts!		
Tybalt	I will withdraw, but this intrusion shall		
	Now seeming sweet, convert to bitter gall. *He exits.*		
Romeo	*[To Juliet.]* If I profane with my unworthiest hand	**35**	
	This holy shrine, the gentle sin is this,		
	My lips, two blushing pilgrims, ready stand		
	To smooth that rough touch with a tender kiss.		
Juliet	Good pilgrim, you do wrong your hand too much,		
	Which mannerly devotion shows in this,	**40**	
	For saints have hands, that pilgrims' hands do touch,		
	And palm to palm is holy palmers' kiss.		
Romeo	Have not saints lips, and holy palmers too?		
Juliet	Ay, pilgrim, lips that they must use in prayer.		
Romeo	O, then, dear saint, let lips do what hands do;	**45**	
	They pray (grant thou) lest faith turn to despair.		
Juliet	Saints do not move, though grant for prayers' sake.		
Romeo	Then move not, while my prayer's effect I take.		
	They kiss.		
	Thus from my lips, by thine, my sin is purged		
Juliet	Then have my lips the sin that they have took.	**50**	
Romeo	Sin from my lips? O trespass sweetly urged!		
	Give me my sin again. *[They kiss again.]*		
Juliet	You kiss by th' book.		
Nurse	Madam, your mother craves a word with you.		
	Juliet moves away.		
Romeo	What is her mother?		

18 **in spite:** showing us no respect

22 **Content thee:** don't be so angry
23 **'A bears him like a portly gentleman:** he's behaving perfectly well
24 **note:** notice

27 **goodman boy:** an insult suggesting Tybalt isn't behaving like a gentleman

29 **'tis a shame:** it brings shame on us
29 **Go to!:** that's enough of this
30 **saucy:** disgracefully rude. For the next few lines, Capulet is talking to his guests, his servants and Tybalt in quick succession
35 **profane:** mistreat a holy object
36 **This holy shrine:** Juliet's hand
37 **pilgrims:** travellers to holy places

39 **you do wrong:** you are unkind to
40 **mannerly devotion … this:** is acting with proper respect
43 **palmers:** name for pilgrims to the Holy Land, who came back with a palm leaf
43 **palm to palm is holy palmers' kiss:** it's more appropriate for palmers to touch hands in greeting, not kiss
47 **grant for prayers' sake:** they answer prayers
48 **my prayer's effect:** a kiss
49 **purged:** cleaned away

51 **urged:** argued for

52 **You kiss by th' book:** in just the right way

54–**What:** who

Juliet and the Nurse
Was this photograph taken
before or after line 61?

Nurse	Marry, bachelor,	
	Her mother is the lady of the house.	55
Romeo	*[Aside.]* Is she a Capulet?	
	O dear account! My life is my foe's debt.	
Benvolio	Away, begone, the sport is at the best.	
Romeo	Ay, so I fear; the more is my unrest.	

They all exit, except Juliet and the Nurse.

Juliet	Come hither, nurse. What is yond gentleman?	60
Nurse	His name is Romeo, and a Montague;	
	The only son of your great enemy.	
Juliet	My only love sprung from my only hate!	
	Too early seen unknown, and known too late.	
Nurse	What's this? what's this?	65
Juliet	A rhyme I learned even now	
	Of one I danced withal.	

Someone calls within, "Juliet!".

| Nurse | Anon, anon! | |
| | Come let's away, the strangers all are gone. *They exit.* | |

57 dear account: what a high price

57 My life … debt: an enemy holds my life in her hands

58 the sport … best: we've had the best of it

59 the more is my unrest: that's what bothers me

60 yond: over there

63 sprung from …hate: born into my enemy's family

64 Too early … too late: I fell in love before I knew who he was

Stage direction within: coming from 'off stage' in the tiring house behind the stage

67 Anon: I'm on my way

68 strangers: people who don't live in the house

These questions ask you to reflect on all of Act 1.

a) How do Romeo's language and the imagery he uses during Act 1 show the difference between how he feels about Rosaline and his feelings when he meets Juliet?

b) How should the actor playing Romeo show his different feelings through Act 1?

c) How is the importance of family loyalty shown in the events of Act 1?

d) How is the theme of fate developed during Act 1?

e) What impression does an audience have of both Romeo and Juliet by the end of Act 1?

Romeo, as he first sees Juliet on the balcony, Act 2 Scene 2, lines 4–6.
Actors often talk about Shakespeare giving them instructions about what to do in the words characters speak in the play. What 'stage directions in text' are there in these lines?

Upper Level

Actors in Shakespeare's theatres used more than just the stage. A trapdoor in the stage let them come up onto, or disappear below, the stage. There was also an upper level above the stage, at about the same height as the middle gallery seats. It was small and often crowded, as it contained not only the most expensive audience seats but also the musicians. For this reason, scenes on the Upper Level are usually short and have no more than three characters. Actors used the Upper Level for scenes where a character can watch others unseen, or is somewhere actually higher, such as on the walls of a city. The 'balcony scene' in Romeo and Juliet is unusually long. However, only Juliet is on the upper level (Romeo says she is 'o'er my head' in line 10), and she does not need to move much.

Act 2 Scene 1

Enter Romeo alone.

Romeo	Can I go forward when my heart is here?
	Turn back, dull earth, and find thy centre out.

Enter Benvolio with Mercutio. Romeo hides.

Benvolio	Romeo! My cousin Romeo! Romeo!
Mercutio	On my life hath stol'n him home to bed.
Benvolio	He ran this way and leapt this orchard wall. **5**
	Call, good Mercutio.
Mercutio	Nay, I'll conjure too.
	Romeo! Humours! Madman! Passion! Lover!
	I conjure thee by Rosaline's bright eyes,
	By her high forehead and her scarlet lip,
	By her fine foot, straight leg and quivering thigh, **10**
	And the demesnes that there adjacent lie,
	That in thy likeness thou appear to us.
Benvolio	Come, he hath hid himself among these trees
	To be consorted with the humorous night.
	Blind is his love and best befits the dark. **15**
Mercutio	If love be blind, love cannot hit the mark.
	Come, shall we go?
Benvolio	Go, then; for 'tis in vain
	To seek him here that means not to be found.

Exit Mercutio and Benvolio.

1 **go forward:** walk away
2 **dull earth:** my body
2 **thy centre:** his heart, with Juliet

6 **conjure too:** magic him out of the air
7 **Humours:** moody one

11 **demesnes:** places
11 **adjacent:** nearby

14 **To be consorted:** be alone with
14 **humorous:** double meaning: damp; moody
16 **the mark:** what it aims at

Act 2 Scene 2

Romeo steps out.

Romeo	He jests at scars that never felt a wound.
	But, soft, what light through yonder window breaks?
	It is the east and Juliet is the sun.

Enter Juliet above.

	It is my lady, O it is my love!
	O that she knew she were! **5**
	See how she leans her cheek upon her hand.
	O that I were a glove upon that hand,
	That I might touch that cheek.
Juliet	Ay me.
Romeo	She speaks!
	O speak again, bright angel, for thou art
	As glorious to this night, being o'er my head, **10**
	As is a wingèd messenger of heaven
Juliet	O Romeo, Romeo, wherefore art thou Romeo?

1 **He jests … a wound:** only someone who hasn't been in love can joke about the pain it gives
2 **soft:** hush

5 **O that:** if only

11 **wingèd messenger of heaven:** angel
12 **wherefore art thou:** why are you

Romeo
Was this photograph taken before or after line 38?

Deny thy father and refuse thy name,
Or if thou wilt not, be but sworn my love
And I'll no longer be a Capulet.   15

Romeo   *[Aside.]* Shall I hear more, or shall I speak at this?

Juliet   'Tis but thy name that is my enemy.
Thou art thyself, though not a Montague.
What's Montague? It is nor hand, nor foot,
Nor arm, nor face, nor any other part   20
Belonging to a man. O be some other name!
What's in a name? That which we call a rose
By any other name would smell as sweet.
So Romeo would, were he not Romeo called,
Retain that dear perfection which he owes   25
Without that title. Romeo, doff thy name,
And for that name which is no part of thee
Take all myself.

Romeo   I take thee at thy word.
Call me but love, and I'll be new baptised.
Henceforth I never will be Romeo.   30

Juliet   What man art thou that thus bescreened in night
So stumblest on my counsel?

Romeo   By a name
I know not how to tell thee who I am.
My name, dear saint, is hateful to myself,
Because it is an enemy to thee.   35

Juliet   My ears have not yet drunk a hundred words
Of thy tongue's uttering, yet I know the sound.
Art thou not Romeo, and a Montague?

Romeo   Neither, fair maid, if either thee dislike.

Juliet   How camest thou hither, tell me, and wherefore?   40
The orchard walls are high and hard to climb,
And the place death, considering who thou art,
If any of my kinsmen find thee here.

Romeo   With Love's light wings did I o'erperch these walls,
He lent me counsel and I lent him eyes.   45
I am no pilot, yet, wert thou as far
As that vast shore washed with the farthest sea,
I would adventure for such merchandise.

Juliet   Thou know'st the mask of night is on my face,
Else would a maiden blush bepaint my cheek   50
For that which thou hast heard me speak to-night.
Dost thou love me? I know thou wilt say "Ay,"
And I will take thy word. Yet if thou swear'st,
Thou mayst prove false. At lovers' perjuries,
They say, Jove laughs. O gentle Romeo,   55
If thou dost love, pronounce it faithfully.

---

13 **Deny thy father … thy name:** say you are not a Montague

18 **Thou art … a Montague:** change your name and you will be the same person

25 **owes:** owns
26 **doff:** take off

31 **bescreened in:** hidden by

32 **counsel:** private exploration of my thoughts

37 **Of thy tongue's uttering:** you have spoken
39 **if either thee dislike:** if you don't like either of them
42–3 **the place death … thee here:** as you are a Montague, any Capulet who finds you here will kill you
44 **o'erperch:** fly over
45 **lent me counsel:** advised me
46 **pilot:** navigator that guides ships into harbour
48 **I would … merchandise:** I'd take the risks with you as the reward
50 **Else:** otherwise
54 **perjuries:** broken oaths
55 **Jove:** king of the gods in Roman myths
55 **laughs:** doesn't take seriously, won't punish
56 **pronounce it faithfully:** tell me so truthfully

These questions are about all of Act 2 Scene 2.

1 How do the words and imagery used by Romeo show the audience the love he feels for Juliet?

2 How do the two lovers' words and images develop the theme of love in the play?

3 What do Juliet's words and the decisions she makes tell the audience about her character?

Juliet (above) and Romeo
Why might Shakespeare have chosen to have the lovers separated by a physical barrier in this tender love scene?

Romeo	Lady, by yonder blessed moon I vow, —	
Juliet	O, swear not by the moon, th' inconstant moon,	
	That monthly changes in her circled orb,	
	Lest that thy love prove likewise variable.	**60**
Romeo	What shall I swear by?	
Juliet	Do not swear at all.	
	Or, if thou wilt, swear by thy gracious self,	
	Which is the god of my idolatry,	
	And I'll believe thee.	
Romeo	If my heart's dear love —	
Juliet	Well, do not swear. Although I joy in thee,	**65**
	I have no joy of this contract tonight.	
	It is too rash, too unadvised, too sudden,	
	Too like the lightning, which doth cease to be	
	Ere one can say "It lightens." Sweet, good night.	
	This bud of love, by summer's ripening breath,	**70**
	May prove a beauteous flower when next we meet.	
	Good night, good night, as sweet repose and rest	
	Come to thy heart as that within my breast.	
Romeo	O wilt thou leave me so unsatisfied?	
Juliet	What satisfaction canst thou have tonight?	**75**
Romeo	Th' exchange of thy love's faithful vow for mine.	
Juliet	I gave thee mine before thou didst request it.	
	I hear some noise within. Dear love, adieu. —	

Nurse calls within.

	Anon, good nurse! — Sweet Montague, be true.	
	Stay but a little, I will come again. *Exit Juliet, above.*	
Romeo	O blessèd, blessèd night! I am afeard	**81**
	Being in night, all this is but a dream. *Enter Juliet, above.*	
Juliet	Three words, dear Romeo, and good night indeed,	
	If that thy bent of love be honourable,	
	Thy purpose marriage, send me word tomorrow,	**85**
	By one that I'll procure to come to thee,	
	Where and what time thou wilt perform the rite,	
	And all my fortunes at thy foot I'll lay	
	And follow thee my lord throughout the world.	
Nurse	*[Within.]* Madam!	**90**
Juliet	I come, anon. — But if thou mean'st not well,	
	I do beseech thee —	
Nurse	*[Within.]* Madam!	
Juliet	By and by, I come. —	
	To cease thy strife, and leave me to my grief,	**95**
	Tomorrow will I send.	
Romeo	So thrive my soul —	

58 **inconstant:** ever changing

59 **in her circled orb:** as she moves through the sky

63 **of my idolatory:** I worship

66 **this contract:** these promises we are making

67 **too unadvised:** not thought through

74 **unsatisfied:** double meaning: without having sorted things out; sexually unsatisfied

79 **Anon:** I'm on my way

80 **Stay but a little:** wait just a minute

84 **thy bent of love:** your intentions

85 **Thy purpose:** your aim

86 **procure:** set up

87 **the rite:** the wedding ceremony

91 **thou mean'st not well:** you don't mean marriage, just seduction

92 **beseech:** beg

94 **By and by:** right away

95 **thy strife:** trying to make me love you

95 **leave me to my grief:** grief because he doesn't mean to marry her

Friar Lawrence
What impression of Friar Lawrence do you get from this photograph?

Juliet	A thousand times good night!
Romeo	A thousand times the worse to want thy light.

Exit Juliet, above.

Love goes toward love as schoolboys from their books,
But love from love, toward school with heavy looks. **100**

Enter Juliet, above, again.

Juliet	Romeo, what o'clock tomorrow Shall I send to thee?
Romeo	By the hour of nine.
Juliet	I will not fail, 'tis twenty years till then. I have forgot why I did call thee back.
Romeo	Let me stand here till thou remember it. **105**
Juliet	'Tis almost morning, I would have thee gone. Good night, good night! Parting is such sweet sorrow, That I shall say good night till it be morrow.

Exit Juliet, above.

Romeo	Sleep dwell upon thine eyes, peace in thy breast, Would I were sleep and peace, so sweet to rest. **110** Hence will I to my ghostly Friar's close cell, His help to crave, and my dear hap to tell. *He exits.*

Act 2 Scene 3

Enter Friar Lawrence, with a basket.

Friar Lawrence	Now, ere the sun advance his burning eye, The day to cheer and night's dank dew to dry, I must upfill this osier cage of ours With baleful weeds and precious-juicèd flowers.

Enter Romeo.

Romeo	Good morrow, father.
Friar Lawrence	*Benedicite.* **5** What early tongue so sweet saluteth me? Young son, it argues a distempered head So soon to bid good morrow to thy bed. Thou art up-roused by some distemp'rature. Or if not so, then here I hit it right, **10** Our Romeo hath not been in bed tonight.
Romeo	That last is true, the sweeter rest was mine.
Friar Lawrence	God pardon sin! Wast thou with Rosaline?
Romeo	With Rosaline, my ghostly father? No, I have forgot that name and that name's woe. **15**
Friar Lawrence	That's my good son, but where hast thou been then?
Romeo	I'll tell thee, ere thou ask it me again.

98 the worse to want thy light: darker without you to light it

111 Hence will I: I'll go from here

111 ghostly Friar's close cell: the private room of Friar Lawrence, Romeo's 'spiritual' father

112 crave: ask for

112 my dear hap: my good luck

1 ere: before

3 upfill this osier cage: fill my willow basket

4 baleful weeds: poisonous herbs

5 *Benedicite*: God bless you

7 argues a distempered head: suggests something is troubling you

9 up-roused … distemp'rature: out of bed because you're troubled

12 the sweeter … mine: I was doing something better than sleeping

14 ghostly father: spiritual father, religious teacher

15 that name's woe: the misery it gave me

These questions are about all of Act 2 Scene 3.

1 How do the words and imagery used by Friar Lawrence emphasise the need to act slowly and not to rush in to the marriage?

2 If you were directing the play, how would you tell the actor playing Friar Lawrence to move and speak to make a contrast with Romeo?

3 How is Romeo's love made clear in this scene?

4 What impression does an audience have of Friar Lawrence's character from this scene?

Romeo has just been slapped by Friar Lawrence.
Compare this photograph with the one on page 34. That production interpreted the Friar as an old and wise man. In this production he is younger and more aggressive. How do both work with the lines Shakespeare gave the Friar to say?

36

	I have been feasting with mine enemy,	
	Where on a sudden one hath wounded me	
	That's by me wounded. Both our remedies	20
	Within thy help and holy physic lies.	
Friar Lawrence	Be plain, good son, and homely in thy drift,	
	Riddling confession finds but riddling shrift.	
Romeo	Then plainly know my heart's dear love is set	
	On the fair daughter of rich Capulet.	25
	As mine on hers, so hers is set on mine.	
	When and where and how	
	We met, we wooed and made exchange of vow,	
	I'll tell thee as we pass. But this I pray,	
	That thou consent to marry us today.	30
Friar Lawrence	Holy Saint Francis, what a change is here!	
	Is Rosaline, that thou didst love so dear,	
	So soon forsaken? Young men's love then lies	
	Not truly in their hearts, but in their eyes.	
Romeo	Thou chid'st me oft for loving Rosaline.	35
Friar Lawrence	For doting, not for loving, pupil mine.	
Romeo	And bad'st me bury love.	
Friar Lawrence	Not in a grave	
	To lay one in, another out to have.	
Romeo	I pray thee, chide me not. Her I love now	
	Doth grace for grace, and love for love allow.	40
	The other did not so.	
Friar Lawrence	O she knew well	
	Thy love did read by rote, that could not spell.	
	But come young waverer, come, go with me,	
	In one respect I'll thy assistant be.	
	For this alliance may so happy prove,	45
	To turn your households' rancour to pure love.	
Romeo	O let us hence. I stand on sudden haste.	
Friar Lawrence	Wisely and slow, they stumble that run fast. *They exit.*	

Act 2 Scene 4

Enter Benvolio and Mercutio.

Mercutio	Where the devil should this Romeo be?	
	Came he not home tonight?	
Benvolio	Not to his father's, I spoke with his man.	
Mercutio	Why that same pale hard-hearted wench, that Rosaline,	
	Torments him so, that he will sure run mad.	5
Benvolio	Tybalt, the kinsman of old Capulet,	
	Hath sent a letter to his father's house.	

20–1 Both our ... physic lies: you can cure us both by helping us and using your religious powers

22 Be plain: make your meaning clear

22 homely in thy drift: use simple language

23 Riddling confession ... shrift: your confession has to be properly understood to be properly pardoned

29 pass: walk along

35 chid'st: were angry with me

36 doting: being infatuated

38 To lay one ... to have: to bury one love in and take another from

40 grace for grace, and love for love allow: loves me equally

42 read ... not spell: just going through the motions, not real

44 In one respect: for one reason

45 this alliance: your marriage

46 rancour: deep-rooted enmity

47 I stand on sudden haste: I'm in a hurry

What's just happened

- It is the morning after the Capulets' party.
- Mercutio and Benvolio could not find Romeo after the party, and they still cannot find him in the morning.

1 should: can

3 his father's: Romeo's father's

Mercutio and Benvolio
Does the photograph suggest Mercutio and Benvolio are serious young men, or boisterous young men who mess about a lot? How well does this fit the text of this scene?

Mercutio	A challenge, on my life.
Benvolio	Romeo will answer it.
Mercutio	Alas poor Romeo, he is already dead: run through the ear with a love song, the very pin of his heart cleft with the blind bow-boy's butt-shaft. And is he a man to encounter Tybalt?
Benvolio	Why, what is Tybalt?
Mercutio	More than prince of cats. O he's the courageous captain of compliments. He fights as you sing prick-song, keeps time, distance and proportion. Ah, the immortal *passado*, the *punto reverso*, *the hay*.
Benvolio	The what?
Mercutio	The pox of such antic, lisping, affecting fantasticoes, these new tuners of accent!

Enter Romeo.

Benvolio	Here comes Romeo, here comes Romeo.
Mercutio	Signior Romeo, *bonjour*. You gave us the counterfeit fairly last night.
Romeo	Good morrow to you both. What counterfeit did I give you?
Mercutio	The slip, sir, the slip. Can you not conceive?
Romeo	Pardon, good Mercutio, my business was great, and in such a case as mine a man may strain courtesy.
Mercutio	That's as much as to say, such a case as yours constrains a man to bow in the hams.
Romeo	Meaning, to courtesy.
Mercutio	Thou hast most kindly hit it.
Romeo	A most courteous exposition.
Mercutio	Nay, I am the very pink of courtesy.

Enter Nurse and Peter.

Romeo	Here's goodly gear.
Nurse	Peter!
Peter	Anon.
Nurse	My fan, Peter.
Mercutio	Good Peter, to hide her face! For her fan's the fairer face!
Nurse	God you good morrow, gentlemen.
Mercutio	God you good e'en, fair gentlewoman.
Nurse	Is it good e'en?
Mercutio	'Tis no less, I tell you, for the bawdy hand of the dial is now upon the prick of noon.

Line numbers: 10, 15, 20, 25, 30, 35, 41, 45

8 A challenge, on my life: I bet it's a challenge to a duel
9 answer: accept
11 pin of his heart: heart's centre
11 cleft: split
12 the blind bow-boy's: Cupid's
12 butt-shaft: blunt, target practice arrow
13 encounter: fight a duel with
14 what is: what kind of a man is
15 prince of cats: refers to Tybert, prince of cats in a well-known story at the time
16 captain of compliments: master of all the latest rules of fighting
16–7 sing prick-song: sight read sheet music; start of a run of comparisons between duelling and singing.
18 *passado ... hay*: fencing terms
20–1 the pox of ... tuners of accent: curse these affected people with their put-on accents (he then imitates them)
23 gave us the counterfeit: tricked us
27 the slip: double meaning: fake coin; avoiding them
27 conceive: work out what I mean
29 strain courtesy: be rude
30–1 such a case ... in the hams: you're so tired from sex you're weak at the knees
33 Thou hast most kindly hit it: that's right
35 pink: a garden flower; 'flower' was used to refer to virginity, male and female
36 goodly gear: new material for joking
41 God you good morrow: Good morning
42 e'en: any time after noon
44 bawdy: sexually explicit
44 dial: sundial

The Nurse and Mercutio
Does this photograph best fit line 53 or line 57?

These questions are about all of Act 2 Scene 4.

1 How do the words and imagery used by Mercutio show that he is insulting the Nurse?

2 Mercutio makes inappropriate sexual comments to the Nurse. How do these contrast with the love that Romeo and Juliet feel for each other?

Nurse	Out upon you! Gentlemen, can any of you tell me where I may find the young Romeo?	46 **Out upon you:** for shame
Romeo	I can tell you. But young Romeo will be older when you have found him than he was when you sought him. I am the youngest of that name, for fault of a worse. **50**	
Nurse	If you be he, sir, I desire some confidence with you.	
Benvolio	She will endite him to some supper.	52 **endite:** deliberate mistake for 'invite'
Mercutio	A bawd, a bawd, a bawd. So ho! Romeo, will you come to your father's? We'll to dinner thither. **55**	53 **bawd:** woman who runs a brothel 53 **So ho!:** a hunting call 54 **dinner:** the midday meal
Romeo	I will follow you.	
Mercutio	Farewell, ancient lady. Farewell lady, lady, lady.	
	Exit Mercutio and Benvolio.	
Nurse	I pray you, sir, what saucy merchant was this, that was so full of his ropery?	58 **saucy merchant:** rude, un-gentlemanly man 59 **ropery:** spiteful and sexual jokes
Romeo	A gentleman, nurse, that loves to hear himself talk **60** and will speak more in a minute than he will stand to in a month.	63 **An a:** and if he 63 **take him down:** take him down a peg or two
Nurse	An a' speak anything against me, I'll take him down. *[To Peter.]* And thou must stand by too, and suffer every knave to use me at his pleasure? **65**	64 **suffer:** allow 65 **use me at his pleasure:** take advantage of me (unintentional double meaning)
Peter	I saw no man use you at his pleasure. If I had, my weapon should quickly have been out.	
Nurse	Now, afore God, I am so vexed that every part about me quivers. Scurvy knave! *[To Romeo.]* Pray you, sir, a word. And as I told you, my young lady bid me **70** enquire you out. What she bid me say, I will keep to myself. But first let me tell ye, if you should deal double with her, truly it were an ill thing to be offered to any gentlewoman, and very weak dealing.	72 **deal double:** deceive 74 **weak dealing:** shameful behaviour
Romeo	Nurse, commend me to thy lady and mistress. I protest **75** unto thee —	75 **commend me:** give my greetings to 75–6 **I protest unto thee:** I assure you
Nurse	Good heart, and i' faith, I will tell her as much. Lord, Lord, she will be a joyful woman.	
Romeo	Bid her devise some means to come to shrift this afternoon, and there she shall at Friar Lawrence's cell **80** be shrived and married. *[He offers her money.]* Here is for thy pains.	79 **devise some means:** find a way to 79 **shrift:** confession, where she tells her sins to a Catholic priest or friar 81 **be shrived:** have her sins forgiven
Nurse	No truly sir; not a penny.	
Romeo	Go to, I say you shall.	
Nurse	This afternoon, sir? Well, she shall be there. **85**	
Romeo	Farewell, commend me to thy mistress. *Romeo exits.*	
Nurse	Ay, a thousand times. *They exit.*	

What's just happened

- It is the morning after the Capulets' party.
- Juliet has sent the Nurse to meet Romeo.

What is she hoping for?

1 How do the words and imagery used by Juliet in this scene emphasise her need to hear the Nurse's news of Romeo?

2 How should the actor playing the Nurse move and speak to show that she is building up the suspense for Juliet?

Juliet and the Nurse
Does this photograph best fit lines 20–21, or lines 25–6?

Act 2 Scene 5

Enter Juliet.

Juliet	The clock struck nine when I did send the nurse,
	In half an hour she promised to return.
	Perchance she cannot meet him. That's not so.
	O, she is lame.
	Had she affections and warm youthful blood, **5**
	She would be as swift in motion as a ball.
	My words would bandy her to my sweet love,
	And his to me.
	But old folks, many feign as they were dead,
	Unwieldy, slow, heavy, and pale as lead. **10**

Enter Nurse and Peter.

	O God, she comes! O honey nurse, what news?
	Hast thou met with him? Send thy man away.
Nurse	Peter, stay at the gate. *He exits.*
Juliet	Now good sweet nurse — O Lord, why look'st thou sad?
	Though news be sad, yet tell them merrily. **15**
Nurse	I am a-weary, give me leave awhile.
	Fie, how my bones ache! What a jaunce have I had!
Juliet	I would thou hadst my bones, and I thy news.
	Nay, come I pray thee, speak good, good nurse, speak.
Nurse	Jesu, what haste! Can you not stay awhile? **20**
	Do you not see that I am out of breath?
Juliet	How art thou out of breath, when thou hast breath
	To say to me that thou art out of breath?
	Let me be satisfied, is't good or bad?
Nurse	Lord, how my head aches! What a head have I! **25**
	My back a' t'other side. Ah, my back, my back!
	Beshrew your heart for sending me about
	To catch my death with jauncing up and down.
Juliet	I' faith, I am sorry that thou art not well.
	Sweet, sweet, sweet nurse, tell me what says my love? **30**
Nurse	Your love says, like an honest gentleman,
	And a courteous, and a kind, and a handsome,
	And I warrant a virtuous — Where is your mother?
Juliet	Where is my mother? Why, she is within,
	Where should she be? How oddly thou repliest. **35**
	"Your love says, like an honest gentleman,
	Where is your mother?"
Nurse	O God's lady dear,
	Henceforward do your messages yourself.

3   **Perchance:** perhaps
7   **bandy:** hit her (like a tennis ball)
9   **feign as:** act as if

13   **stay:** wait

16   **give me leave awhile:** just wait a minute
17   **jaunce:** exhausting trip

26   **a' t' other side:** on the other side
27   **Beshrew:** curse
28   **jauncing:** prancing like a horse

31   **honest:** honourable

34   **within:** indoors

37   **God's lady dear:** Mary, Christ's mother
38   **Henceforward:** from now on

These questions ask you to reflect on all of Act 2.

a) How do the words and imagery used in Act 2 make the love of Romeo and Juliet feel real and powerful?

b) How is the theme of love developed in the events which take place in Act 2?

c) How important is it to understand the way society in Shakespeare's time expected marriages to take place when thinking about the events of Act 2?

d) How important are the actions of the Nurse and Friar Lawrence in the events of Act 2?

Juliet, Friar Lawrence and Romeo
How do the words and imagery of death, violence and sorrow fit with the lovers preparing for marriage?

Juliet	Here's such a coil. Come, what says Romeo?
Nurse	Have you got leave to go to shrift to-day? **40**
Juliet	I have.
Nurse	Then hie you hence to Friar Lawrence's cell,
	There stays a husband to make you a wife.
	Hie you to church, I must another way,
	To fetch a ladder by the which your love **45**
	Must climb a bird's nest soon when it is dark.
	I am the drudge and toil in your delight,
	But you shall bear the burden soon at night.
	Go, I'll to dinner, hie you to the cell.
Juliet	Hie to high fortune! Honest nurse, farewell. **50**

They exit.

Act 2 Scene 6

Enter Friar Lawrence and Romeo.

Friar Lawrence	So smile the heavens upon this holy act,
	That after hours with sorrow chide us not!
Romeo	Do thou but close our hands with holy words,
	Then love-devouring death do what he dare,
	It is enough I may but call her mine. **5**
Friar Lawrence	These violent delights have violent ends
	And in their triumph, die like fire and powder,
	Which as they kiss consume.
	Therefore love moderately, long love doth so,
	Too swift arrives as tardy as too slow. **10**

Juliet runs in and embraces Romeo.

	Here comes the lady. O so light a foot.
Juliet	Good even to my ghostly confessor.
Friar Lawrence	Romeo shall thank thee, daughter, for us both.
Romeo	Ah, Juliet, if the measure of thy joy
	Be heaped like mine, then sweeten with thy breath **15**
	This neighbour air, and let rich music's tongue
	Unfold the imagined happiness that both
	Receive in either by this dear encounter.
Juliet	But my true love is grown to such excess
	I cannot sum up sum of half my wealth. **20**
Friar Lawrence	Come, come with me, and we will make short work.
	For, by your leaves, you shall not stay alone
	Till holy church incorporate two in one.

They all exit.

39 **coil:** fuss

44 **hie you hence:** go

47 **drudge:** poor, unimportant servant
48 **bear the burden:** carry the weight of Romeo during sex

What's just happened
- Romeo told the Nurse that he will meet Juliet at Friar Lawrence's cell to marry her.
- The Nurse has given Juliet the message.

What are Juliet and Romeo feeling?

2 **after hours … chide us not:** we aren't punished by sorrow in the future
3 **Do thou but … holy words:** Just marry us
7 **powder:** gunpowder
8 **as they kiss consume:** burn each other up on touching
10 **tardy:** late
12 **ghostly:** spiritual
12 **confessor:** priest or friar who hears a person confess their sins
14–5 **the measure … heaped like mine:** if you're as happy as I am
16 **This neighbour air:** the air around us
17 **Unfold:** tell
17–8 **both Receive in either:** we both will have
20 **sum up sum:** calculate
21 **make short work:** quickly marry you
23 **incorporate two in one:** has made you husband and wife

What's just happened

- Tension between the Montagues and Capulets is high.
- Tybalt (Capulet) feels that Romeo deliberately insulted his family by gatecrashing their feast.
- Romeo has (secretly) married Juliet, and now feels very differently about the Capulets.

How do Tybalt and Romeo feel about each other?

Romeo (back to camera) and Tybalt
What do Tybalt's expression and body language suggest about his feelings towards Romeo?

Act 3 Scene 1

Enter Benvolio, Mercutio, his page, and servants of the Montagues.

Benvolio	I pray thee, good Mercutio, let's retire,
	The day is hot, the Capels are abroad,
	And if we meet we shall not 'scape a brawl.
Mercutio	Thou art like one of those fellows, that when he enters
	the confines of a tavern, claps me his sword upon the **5**
	table and says "God send me no need of thee", and by
	the operation of the second cup, draws him on the
	drawer, when indeed there is no need.
Benvolio	Am I like such a fellow?
Mercutio	Thou? Why thou wilt quarrel with a man that hath a **10**
	hair more, or a hair less, in his beard than thou hast.
	And yet thou wilt tutor me from quarrelling?
Benvolio	And I were so apt to quarrel as thou art, any man should
	buy the fee-simple of my life for an hour and a quarter.
Mercutio	The fee-simple? O simple! **15**

Enter Tybalt, Petruchio, and others.

Benvolio	By my head, here comes the Capulets.
Mercutio	By my heel, I care not.
Tybalt	Gentlemen, good e'en, a word with one of you.
Mercutio	And but one word with one of us? Couple it with
	something, make it a word and a blow. **20**
Tybalt	You shall find me apt enough to that, sir, and you will
	give me occasion.
Mercutio	Could you not take some occasion without giving?
Tybalt	Mercutio, thou consortest with Romeo.
Mercutio	Consort? What, dost thou make us minstrels? And thou **25**
	make minstrels of us, look to hear nothing but discords.
	[Moving his hand to his sword.] Here's my fiddlestick,
	here's that shall make you dance. 'Zounds, consort!
Benvolio	We talk here in the public haunt of men.
	Either withdraw unto some private place, **30**
	Or reason coldly of your grievances,
	Or else depart. Here all eyes gaze on us.
Mercutio	Men's eyes were made to look, and let them gaze.
	I will not budge for no man's pleasure, I.

Enter Romeo.

Tybalt	Well, peace be with you, sir, here comes my man. **35**
	Romeo, the love I bear thee can afford
	No better term than this: thou art a villain.

1   **retire:** go home
2   **Capels:** Capulets
2   **abroad:** somewhere around
3   **'scape a brawl:** be able to avoid a fight
5   **the confines of a tavern:** a pub
5   **claps me his sword:** bangs his sword
7   **the operation … cup:** the time he's had his second drink
7   **draws him:** draws his sword
8   **drawer:** man serving the drink
12   **tutor me from:** advise me to avoid
13   **And I … apt:** if I was so given to
15   **fee-simple:** complete ownership
15   **simple:** fool
16   **By my head:** a common exclamation
17   **By my heel:** made up by Mercutio, hinting at running away
19   **Couple:** join
22   **occasion:** a good reason
24   **consortest with:** are a friend of
25   **minstrels:** music makers – a 'consort' is a small group of musicians
25   **And thou:** if you
27   **fiddlestick:** he means his sword
28   **'Zounds:** an oath, from 'God's wounds'
29   **the public haunt of men:** a public place
31   **reason coldly of:** calmly talk through
34   **I will not … pleasure:** I won't move for any man's convenience
35   **my man:** the man I'm looking for

Benvolio (left, mainly hidden), Mercutio (brandishing sword), Romeo, Tybalt (stabbing Mercutio).
The modern stage direction (in red) and the action in this photograph are both driven by one of Shakespeare's 'stage directions in text'. What is it?

Swords and swordfighting

In Shakespeare's time, most gentlemen and nobles wore a sword in public, and many had a dagger, too. These weapons were more a sign of status than for defence. In *Romeo and Juliet*, it is a sign of how dangerous the feud between the Capulets and the Montagues had become that even their servants carried swords. Gentlemen were taught to fight with their swords, although they were usually taught fencing. This was fighting with covered sword points (so they were less dangerous) and stressed skill and clever moves rather than injuring or killing your opponent. Fencing also had rules that had to be obeyed, and each move had a name (Mercutio refers to the *passado* in line 55).

Because gentlemen carried swords, the feud between the Montagues and the Capulets could easily turn into deadly fighting. In this scene there is no thought of using swords with covered points.

Spectacular swordfights were a very popular feature of plays at the time, and (as now) many of the actors were highly trained swordfighters.

Romeo	Villain am I none,
	Therefore farewell, I see thou knowest me not.
Tybalt	Boy, this shall not excuse the injuries **40**
	That thou hast done me, therefore turn and draw.
Romeo	I do protest I never injured thee,
	But love thee better than thou canst devise
	Till thou shalt know the reason of my love.
	And so, good Capulet, which name I tender **45**
	As dearly as my own, be satisfied.
Mercutio	O calm, dishonourable, vile submission!

Drawing his sword.

	Tybalt, you rat-catcher, will you walk?
Tybalt	What wouldst thou have with me?
Mercutio	Good king of cats, nothing but one of your nine lives. **50**
	Will you pluck your sword out of his pilcher by the ears?
	Make haste, lest mine be about your ears ere it be out.
Tybalt	I am for you. *[Drawing his sword.]*
Romeo	Gentle Mercutio, put thy rapier up.
Mercutio	Come sir, your *passado*. *[They fight.]* **55**
Romeo	Draw, Benvolio; beat down their weapons.
	Gentlemen, for shame, forbear this outrage!
	Tybalt, Mercutio, the Prince expressly hath
	Forbidden bandying in Verona streets:
	Hold, Tybalt! Good Mercutio! **60**

During the fight, Romeo tries to part them, and Tybalt stabs Mercutio under Romeo's arm. Tybalt runs offstage.

Mercutio	I am hurt.
	A plague on both your houses! I am sped.
	Is he gone and hath nothing?
Benvolio	What, art thou hurt?
Mercutio	Ay, ay, a scratch, a scratch. Marry, 'tis enough. **65**
	Fetch a surgeon. *Exit Page.*
Romeo	Courage man, the hurt cannot be much.
Mercutio	No, 'tis not so deep as a well, nor so wide as a church
	door; but 'tis enough, 'twill serve. Ask for me
	tomorrow, and you shall find me a grave man. **70**
	A plague o' both your houses! Why the devil came
	you between us? I was hurt under your arm.
Romeo	I thought all for the best.
Mercutio	Help me into some house, Benvolio,
	Or I shall faint. A plague o' both your houses! **75**
	They have made worms' meat of me.

Glossary notes:

40 **Boy:** an insult to a young man
41 **turn and draw:** come back and fight
43 **devise:** imagine

45 **tender:** value
46 **be satisfied:** don't push this challenge

48 **will you walk:** will you fight me

51 **pilcher:** scabbard
51 **by the ears:** right now, with no formality
52 **lest:** in case

55 *passado*: fencing term

57 **forbear:** stop

59 **bandying:** fighting

62 **A plague on both your houses:** [he is cursing both Montagues and Capulets]
62 **sped:** fatally wounded
63 **Is he gone … nothing?:** has Tybalt got away unwounded?
65 **'tis enough:** it's enough to kill me

69 **'twill serve:** it's enough to kill me
70 **grave:** double meaning: serious; dead

76 **worms' meat:** a corpse

1 How does the action in this scene add to the theme of the hatred between the two families?

2 What is the effect of the blood on Lady Capulet's hand?

Lady Capulet kneels over the body of Tybalt. This photograph was taken between lines 101–104. Who do you think Lady Capulet is looking at?

	I have it, and soundly too. Your houses!		**77**	**I have it, and soundly too:** I'm certainly fatally wounded

Mercutio exits, helped by Benvolio and the servants.

Romeo   This gentleman hath got his mortal hurt
In my behalf. O sweet Juliet,
Thy beauty hath made me effeminate   **80**
And in my temper softened valour's steel.

79 **In my behalf:** defending me

80 **effeminate:** weak, not manly
81 **temper:** double meaning: hardening (as in steel for a sword); nature
81 **softened valour's steel:** made me cowardly

Enter Benvolio.

Benvolio   O Romeo, Romeo, brave Mercutio is dead.

Romeo   This day's black fate on more days doth depend,
This but begins the woe others must end. *[Starting to leave.]*

83 **on more … depend:** will affect the future
84 **others:** other days

Benvolio   Here comes the furious Tybalt back again. *[Enter Tybalt.]*

Romeo   Alive in triumph and Mercutio slain?   **86**
Away to heaven respective lenity,
And fire and fury be my conduct now.
Now, Tybalt, take the "villain" back again
That late thou gav'st me, for Mercutio's soul   **90**
Is but a little way above our heads,
Staying for thine to keep him company.
Either thou, or I, or both, must go with him.

87 **Away to … lenity:** no more treating him like a relative
88 **be my conduct:** drive my actions
90 **late:** just now

92 **Staying:** waiting

Tybalt   Thou wretched boy, that didst consort him here,
Shalt with him hence.

94 **that didst consort him:** who was with him

Romeo   This shall determine that.   **95**

95 **Shalt with him hence:** will leave with him
95 **This:** [Romeo's sword]

They fight. Tybalt falls.

Benvolio   Romeo, away, be gone!
The citizens are up, and Tybalt slain.
Stand not amazed, the Prince will doom thee death
If thou art taken. Hence, be gone, away!

98 **amazed:** stunned
98 **doom thee:** sentence you to

Romeo   O! I am fortune's fool!

Benvolio   Why dost thou stay?   **100**

100 **fortune's fool:** the puppet of Fortune, the goddess of luck

Exit Romeo, then enter citizens from another door, and Prince, Montague, Capulet, their wives and followers.

Lady Capulet   Tybalt, my cousin! O my brother's child!
O Prince! O cousin! Husband! O, the blood is spilled
Of my dear kinsman. Prince, as thou art true,
For blood of ours, shed blood of Montague.

103 **true:** fair

Prince   Benvolio, who began this bloody fray?   **105**

Benvolio   Tybalt, here slain, whom Romeo's hand did slay.
An envious thrust from Tybalt hit the life
Of stout Mercutio, and then Tybalt fled.
But by and by comes back to Romeo,
And to't they go like lightning, for ere I   **110**

107 **envious:** malicious
107 **hit the life:** killed
109 **by and by:** at that moment
110 **ere:** before

Juliet, during her soliloquy
Shakespeare uses this soliloquy to show the strength of Juliet's passion for Romeo. He also uses it to build the audience's sympathy for her. How does he do this?

	Could draw to part them, was stout Tybalt slain. And as he fell, did Romeo turn and fly. This is the truth, or let Benvolio die.	
Lady Capulet	He is a kinsman to the Montague, Affection makes him false he speaks not true. I beg for justice, which thou, Prince, must give. Romeo slew Tybalt, Romeo must not live.	115
Prince	Romeo slew him, he slew Mercutio. Who now the price of his dear blood doth owe?	
Montague	Not Romeo, Prince, he was Mercutio's friend. His fault concludes but what the law should end, The life of Tybalt.	120
Prince	And for that offence Immediately we do exile him hence. I will be deaf to pleading and excuses; Nor tears nor prayers shall purchase out abuses. Therefore use none. Let Romeo hence in haste, Else, when he is found, that hour is his last. Bear hence this body and attend our will. Mercy but murders, pardoning those that kill.	125

Exit all, some carrying Tybalt's body.

Act 3 Scene 2

Enter Juliet alone.

Juliet	Come gentle night, come loving black-browed night. Give me my Romeo, and when I shall die, Take him and cut him out in little stars, And he will make the face of heaven so fine That all the world will be in love with night, And pay no worship to the garish sun.	5

Enter the Nurse, carrying a rope ladder.

	Now, nurse, what news? Why dost thou wring thy hands?	
Nurse	Ah, welladay! He's dead, he's dead, he's dead! We are undone, lady, we are undone! Alack the day, he's gone, he's killed, he's dead.	10
Juliet	Can heaven be so envious?	
Nurse	Romeo can, Though heav'n cannot. O Romeo, Romeo! Who ever would have thought it? Romeo!	
Juliet	What devil art thou that dost torment me thus? Hath Romeo slain himself? Say thou but "Ay", If he be slain, say "Ay"; or if not, "No."	15

111 draw: draw my sword

111 stout: brave

112 fly: run away

115 Affection … false: he's biased in their favour

119 Who now … doth owe?: So who should pay for that?

121 His fault … should end: his action (killing Tybalt) was the execution you would have ordered for killing Mercutio

123 exile him hence: send him away from Verona, never to return

125 purchase out abuses: buy pardons for these crimes

127 Else: otherwise

127 that hour is his last: he will be executed

128 attend our will: come with me to hear your punishment

129 Mercy but … kill: if I pardon murder it will just lead to more killing

What's just happened

- After her secret marriage, Juliet has gone home.
- All she can think about is Romeo, and how he can be smuggled into her bedroom that night.
- Juliet knows nothing of the fighting.

6 garish: vulgar, over-bright

9 welladay: expression of misery

10 undone: ruined

12 envious: malicious, spiteful

12 Romeo can: [the nurse knows he's killed Tybalt]

16 Ay: triple meaning: yes; the pronoun 'I'; sounds like 'eye' (Juliet uses all these in the next few lines)

Juliet and the Nurse
In this production, this scene was played at the front of the stage while the crime scene tape used in the previous scene was still on stage behind them. Do you think the photograph was taken while they were saying lines 32–5, or lines 48–51?

Nurse	I saw the wound, I saw it with mine eyes,	
	O Tybalt, Tybalt, the best friend I had.	
	That ever I should live to see thee dead!	20
Juliet	What storm is this that blows so contrary?	
	Is Romeo slaughtered? And is Tybalt dead?	
	My dearest cousin, and my dearer lord?	
Nurse	Tybalt is gone and Romeo banishèd,	
	Romeo that killed him, he is banishèd.	25
Juliet	O God! Did Romeo's hand shed Tybalt's blood?	
Nurse	It did, it did, alas the day, it did!	
Juliet	O serpent heart, hid with a flowering face.	
	Did ever dragon keep so fair a cave?	
	Beautiful tyrant, fiend angelical,	30
	Dove-feathered raven! Wolvish-ravening lamb!	
Nurse	These griefs, these woes, these sorrows make me old.	
	Shame come to Romeo!	
Juliet	Blistered be thy tongue	
	For such a wish! He was not born to shame.	
	Upon his brow shame is ashamed to sit.	35
	O what a beast was I to chide at him!	
Nurse	Will you speak well of him that killed your cousin?	
Juliet	Shall I speak ill of him that is my husband?	
	Ah, poor my lord, what tongue shall smooth thy name	
	When I, thy three-hours wife, have mangled it?	40
	My husband lives, that Tybalt would have slain;	
	And Tybalt's dead, that would have slain my husband.	
	All this is comfort, wherefore weep I then?	
	Where is my father and my mother, Nurse?	
Nurse	Weeping and wailing over Tybalt's corse.	45
	Will you go to them? I will bring you thither.	
Juliet	Wash they his wounds with tears, mine shall be spent,	
	When theirs are dry, for Romeo's banishment.	
	Death, not Romeo, take my maidenhead.	
Nurse	Hie to your chamber. I'll find Romeo	50
	To comfort you, I wot well where he is.	
Juliet	O find him! Give this ring to my true knight,	
	And bid him come to take his last farewell. *Exit both.*	

23 lord: husband
24 banishèd: forced to leave Verona and not return

28 serpent: the serpent that tempted Eve in the Bible story
28 flowering: handsome, smiling
29 keep: own, live in
31 dove-feathered raven: raven dressed in a dove's white feathers
31 Wolvish-ravening lamb: lamb that behaves like a wolf

36 chide at him: speak badly of him

39 smooth thy name: restore your reputation

45 corse: corpse
46 bring you thither: take you there

49 maidenhead: virginity

50 Hie: go straight
51 wot: know

These questions are about all of Act 3 Scene 2.

1 How are oxymorons (pairs of words with opposite meanings) such as 'beautiful tyrant' used to show Juliet's confusion over the news she receives from the Nurse?

2 How is the tension between love for a person and love for your family emphasised in this scene?

3 How does the Nurse's behaviour in this scene show how she is struggling to be loyal both to Juliet and to the Capulet family?

Friar Lawrence and Romeo; this photograph was taken at line 5. What feature of modern life have the director and designer used to set the tone for this scene?

What's just happened

- Romeo has killed Tybalt in a fight, and he is hiding in Friar Lawrence's cell.
- Friar Lawrence has gone to find out what punishment the Duke has ordered.

What does Romeo fear?

Act 3 Scene 3

Enter Friar Lawrence.

Lawrence	Romeo, come forth, come forth thou fearful man.
	Affliction is enamoured of thy parts,
	And thou art wedded to calamity. *Enter Romeo.*
Romeo	Father, what news?
Friar Lawrence	I bring thee tidings of the Prince's doom.
Romeo	What less than doomsday is the Prince's doom?
Friar Lawrence	A gentler judgement vanished from his lips,
	Not body's death, but body's banishment.
Romeo	Ha, banishment? Be merciful, say "death".
Friar Lawrence	Hence from Verona art thou banishèd.
	Be patient, for the world is broad and wide.
Romeo	There is no world without Verona walls
	But purgatory, torture, hell itself.
	Hence "banishèd" is banished from the world.
Friar Lawrence	O deadly sin, O rude unthankfulness!
	This is dear mercy, and thou seest it not.
Romeo	'Tis torture, and not mercy. Heav'n is here
	Where Juliet lives, and every cat and dog
	And little mouse, every unworthy thing,
	Live here in heaven and may look on her,
	But Romeo may not, he is banishèd.
Friar Lawrence	Thou fond mad man, hear me a little speak.
Romeo	O thou wilt speak again of banishment.
Friar Lawrence	I'll give thee armour to keep off that word,
	Adversity's sweet milk, philosophy,
	To comfort thee, though thou art banishèd.
Romeo	Yet "banishèd"? Hang up philosophy.
Friar Lawrence	O then I see that mad men have no ears.
Romeo	How should they, when that wise men have no eyes?
Friar Lawrence	Let me dispute with thee of thy estate.
Romeo	Thou canst not speak of that thou dost not feel.
	Wert thou as young as I, Juliet thy love,
	An hour but married, Tybalt murderèd,
	Doting like me and like me banishèd.
	Then mightst thou speak.
	Then mightst thou tear thy hair,
	And fall upon the ground, as I do now,
	Taking the measure of an unmade grave. *[Knocking within.]*

Line numbers: 5, 10, 15, 20, 25, 30, 35

1 **fearful:** frightened
2 **Affliction … thy parts:** misery is attracted to you
3 **calamity:** disaster
5 **tidings:** news
5 **doom:** judgement
6 **doomsday:** the Day of Judgement (death)
7 **vanished:** came
12 **without Verona walls:** outside Verona
13 **But:** except
13 **purgatory:** where Catholics believe the souls of the dead suffered for sin before being allowed into Heaven
14 **Hence "banishèd":** to be banished from Verona
16 **dear:** a valuable
22 **fond:** foolish
25 **Adversity's … philosophy:** the best solution to trouble: the ability to think through the problem and accept it
27 **Yet:** still
27 **Hang up:** put away
29 **when that:** when
30 **Let me dispute with thee of thy estate:** let's discuss your situation
33 **An hour but married:** only married an hour ago
34 **Doting:** deeply in love
38 **Taking the measure of:** measuring out

The Nurse, Friar Lawrence, and Romeo
Which line was being spoken when this photograph
was taken – line 57, line 63 or line 75?

These questions are about all of
Act 3 Scene 3.

1 How does the language about
   heaven and hell show Romeo's
   feelings about being banished
   from Verona?

2 How do Friar Lawrence's
   actions and words in this scene
   show the audience that he is a
   thoughtful and caring man?

3 How does Friar Lawrence's
   speech at the end of the scene
   show that the love of Romeo
   and Juliet may be a way to
   bring the battle between the two
   families to a happy end?

Secret marriages

Romeo and Juliet were young enough to need their parents' consent to
marry. They broke the law in marrying without this consent. Friar Lawrence
also broke the law in performing the ceremony. Even if he had not known
their ages, he would have been expected to ask a couple why they came to
be married with no family or witnesses. In Shakespeare's time the Church
had its own courts. These courts would have declared the marriage illegal
and punished Romeo, Juliet and the Friar.

Friar Lawrence agrees to the secret marriage because he hopes it will stop
the feud between the Montagues and the Capulets. In this scene he tells
Romeo to spend the night with with Juliet before he leaves Verona for his
banishment. This was not for sentimental reasons. The law on marriage at
the time was that a true marriage needed either a public promise to marry or
a church wedding, and for the marriage to be consummated (for the couple
to have sex).Once a marriage was consummated, a court was unlikely to
dissolve it.

Friar Lawrence	Arise, one knocks, good Romeo, hide thyself. Thou wilt be taken. — Stay awhile! — Stand up. *[More knocking.]* — By and by! *[More knocking.]* Who knocks so hard? Whence come you? What's your will?	**40**
Nurse	*[Within.]* Let me come in, and you shall know my errand. I come from Lady Juliet.	
Friar Lawrence	Welcome then. *Enter Nurse.*	
Nurse	O holy Friar, O tell me holy Friar, Where is my lady's lord? Where's Romeo?	**45**
Friar Lawrence	There on the ground, with his own tears made drunk.	
Nurse	O, he is even in my mistress' case, Piteous predicament! Even so lies she, Blubbering and weeping, weeping and blubbering. Stand up, stand up, stand and you be a man: For Juliet's sake, for her sake, rise and stand.	**50**
Romeo	Speak'st thou of Juliet? How is it with her? Doth she not think me an old murderer, Where is she? And how doth she? And what says My concealed lady to our cancelled love?	**55**
Nurse	O, she says nothing, sir, but weeps and weeps, And now falls on her bed, and then starts up, And Tybalt calls, and then on Romeo cries, And then down falls again.	
Romeo	As if that name, Shot from the deadly level of a gun, Did murder her; as that name's cursèd hand Murdered her kinsman. *[Drawing his dagger.]*	**60**
Friar Lawrence	Hold thy desperate hand. Art thou a man? Thy form cries out thou art. Thy tears are womanish, thy wild acts denote The unreasonable fury of a beast. What, rouse thee man, thy Juliet is alive, For whose dear sake thou wast but lately dead. There art thou happy. Go get thee to thy love as was decreed, Ascend her chamber, hence and comfort her. But look thou stay not till the Watch be set, For then thou canst not pass to Mantua, Where thou shalt live, till we can find a time To blaze your marriage, reconcile your friends, Beg pardon of the Prince, and call thee back With twenty hundred thousand times more joy Than thou went'st forth in lamentation.	**65** **70** **75**
Nurse	Here sir, a ring she bid me give you sir. Hie you, make haste, for it grows very late. *Exit Nurse.* **80**	

39 **one:** someone
40 **taken:** arrested
40 **Stay awhile!:** wait a minute (to the person knocking)
41 **By and by!:** I'm on my way (to the person knocking)
42 **Whence:** from where
42 **What's your will?:** what do you want?

48 **even in my mistress' case:** in the same state as my mistress

51 **and you be:** if you are

54 **old:** clever, skilful

56 **My concealed lady:** my secret wife
56 **cancelled:** ended, removed

59 **on Romeo cries:** calls out for Romeo
60 **that name:** Romeo
61 **level:** aim

64 **Thy form … thou art:** you look like one
65 **denote:** show
66 **unreasonable:** not thought through
68 **but lately dead:** trying to kill yourself over
69 **happy:** fortunate
70 **as was decreed:** as you planned
72 **look:** make sure that
72 **till the Watch be set:** until the watchmen go on guard at night
73 **pass:** go out of the city gates
75 **blaze:** tell everyone about
75 **reconcile your friends:** get your families to accept it
78 **lamentation:** sorrow

Juliet and Romeo; the photograph was taken during the first three lines of Act 3 Scene 5. What do you think the characters are feeling?

Romeo	How well my comfort is revived by this.	
Friar Lawrence	Either be gone before the Watch be set,	
	Or by the break of day disguised from hence.	
	Give me thy hand, 'tis late. Farewell, good night.	
Romeo	But that a joy past joy calls out on me,	**85**
	It were a grief so brief to part with thee.	
	Farewell.	*They exit.*

85 **calls out on me:** calls me away

86 **It were... with thee:** I'd be sorry to leave you in such a hurry

Act 3 Scene 4

Enter Capulet, Lady Capulet, and Paris.

Capulet	Things have fallen out, sir, so unluckily,	
	That we have had no time to move our daughter.	
	Look you, she loved her kinsman Tybalt dearly,	
	And so did I. Well, we were born to die.	
	'Tis very late, she'll not come down to-night.	**5**
Paris	These times of woe afford no time to woo.	
	Madam, good night, commend me to your daughter.	
Lady Capulet	I will, and know her mind early tomorrow.	
Capulet	Wife, go you to her ere you go to bed,	
	Acquaint her here of my son Paris' love,	**10**
	And bid her, mark you me, on Wednesday next —	
	But soft, what day is this?	
Paris	Monday, my lord.	
Capulet	Monday! Ha, Ha! Well, Wednesday is too soon,	
	O' Thursday let it be. O' Thursday, tell her,	
	She shall be married to this noble earl. —	**15**
	Will you be ready? Do you like this haste?	
Paris	My lord, I would that Thursday were tomorrow.	
Capulet	Well, get you gone, o' Thursday be it, then. —	
	Prepare her wife, against this wedding day. —	
	Farewell, my lord.	*They exit.*

1 **fallen out:** turned out

2 **to move:** to persuade

6 **afford:** give

8 **know her mind:** I'll make her decide

9 **ere:** before

10 **son:** [Capulet has accepted the marriage, so treats Paris as his son-in-law]

11 **bid her:** tell her

11 **mark you me:** listen carefully now

12 **soft:** wait a minute

17 **I would:** I wish

19 **against:** for

What's just happened

- Romeo has managed to get into Juliet's bedroom without being spotted.
- They have spent the night together.

Has this made their position safer, or more dangerous?

Act 3 Scene 5

Enter Romeo and Juliet aloft.

Juliet	Wilt thou be gone? It is not yet near day.	
	It was the nightingale, and not the lark,	
	That pierced the fearful hollow of thine ear.	
Romeo	It was the lark, the herald of the morn,	
	No nightingale.	**5**
	I must be gone and live, or stay and die.	
Juliet	Yond light is not daylight, I know it, I.	
	It is some meteor that the sun exhales	
	To be to thee this night a torch-bearer	
	And light thee on thy way to Mantua.	**10**
	Therefore stay yet, thou need'st not to be gone.	

2 **nightingale/lark:** nightingales sing in the evening, larks sing at dawn

3 **fearful:** frightened

8 **exhales:** breathes out

Juliet and Romeo (on the Upper Level).
Was this photograph more likely to have been taken before or after the Nurse exits (line 30)?

1 How do the words and imagery about the dawn and daylight show the lovers' desperation that they are to be parted?

Romeo	Let me be ta'en, let me be put to death,
	I am content, so thou wilt have it so.
	I'll say yon grey is not the morning's eye,
	Nor that is not the lark whose notes do beat **15**
	The vaulty heaven so high above our heads.
	I have more care to stay than will to go.
	Come death and welcome, Juliet wills it so.
	How is't, my soul? Let's talk, it is not day.
Juliet	It is, it is, hie hence, be gone, away. **20**
	It is the lark that sings so out of tune,
	Straining harsh discords and unpleasing sharps.
	Some say the lark makes sweet division.
	This doth not so, for she divideth us.
	O now be gone. More light and light it grows. **25**
Romeo	More light and light, more dark and dark our woes!

Enter Nurse below.

Nurse	Madam!
Juliet	Nurse?
Nurse	Your lady mother is coming to your chamber.
	The day is broke, be wary, look about. *She exits.* **30**
Juliet	Then window let day in, and let life out.
Romeo	Farewell, farewell. One kiss and I'll descend.

He climbs down.

Juliet	O think'st thou we shall ever meet again?
Romeo	I doubt it not, and all these woes shall serve
	For sweet discourses in our time to come. **35**
Juliet	O God! I have an ill-divining soul.
	Methinks I see thee now, thou art so low,
	As one dead in the bottom of a tomb.
	Either my eyesight fails, or thou look'st pale.
Romeo	And trust me love, in my eye so do you. **40**
	Dry sorrow drinks our blood. Adieu, adieu. *He exits.*
Juliet	Be fickle, Fortune,
	For then I hope thou wilt not keep him long,
	But send him back. *Enter Lady Capulet below.*
Lady Capulet	Ho daughter, are you up?
Juliet	Who is't that calls? — It is my lady mother. **45**
Lady Capulet	Why how now, Juliet?
Juliet	Madam, I am not well.
Lady Capulet	Evermore weeping for your cousin's death?
	What, wilt thou wash him from his grave with tears?
	An if thou couldst, thou couldst not make him live.
	Therefore have done. **50**

12 **ta'en:** taken, arrested
13 **so thou … it so:** if that's what you want
15 **Nor that is not:** and that is not
16 **vaulty:** dome-like
17 **care:** desire

20 **hie hence:** hurry away from here
22 **sharps:** sharp musical notes
23 **sweet division:** a quick run of musical notes

34–5 **all these woes … to come:** we'll talk about these sorrows in the future
36 **I have an ill-divining soul:** I feel in my soul that bad things will happen
37 **so low:** so far down [the ladder]

41 **Dry:** thirsty

42 **fickle:** changeable

46 **how now:** what's wrong

50 **have done:** stop weeping

Capulet cradles Juliet in his arms, lines 89–90.
Who is Capulet looking at?

Family life

In Shakespeare's time, family life had a set structure. Fathers were the head of the household (all the family and the servants living and working in the house). The Church said that children should obey their parents, wives should obey their husbands and servants should obey their master and mistress. Wives ran the home; men went out into the world. Only men could vote, go to university or become doctors or lawyers. However, they were responsible for taking care of the whole household. This included finding husbands for their daughters, because marriage was the only 'career' for a young woman, especially a young woman from a wealthy and important family.

Lady Capulet, Juliet and all the servants were expected to obey Capulet without question. It was shocking that Juliet (a girl not yet fourteen) would question her father's decision, let alone refuse to accept it.

Juliet	Yet let me weep, for such a feeling loss.	
Lady Capulet	Well, girl, thou weep'st not so much for his death, As that the villain lives which slaughtered him.	
Juliet	What villain, madam?	
Lady Capulet	That same villain, Romeo.	
Juliet	[Aside.] Villain and he be many miles asunder. — God pardon him! I do, with all my heart, And yet no man like he doth grieve my heart.	55
Lady Capulet	That is because the traitor murderer lives.	
Juliet	Ay, madam, from the reach of these my hands. Would none but I might venge my cousin's death.	60
Lady Capulet	We will have vengeance for it, fear thou not, And then I hope thou wilt be satisfied.	
Juliet	Indeed I never shall be satisfied With Romeo till I behold him, dead. Madam, if you could find out but a man To bear a poison, I would temper it, That Romeo should, upon receipt thereof, Soon sleep in quiet.	65
Lady Capulet	Find thou the means, and I'll find such a man. But now I'll tell thee joyful tidings, girl.	70
Juliet	What are they, I beseech your ladyship?	
Lady Capulet	Well, well, thou hast a careful father, child! One who, to put thee from thy heaviness, Hath sorted out a sudden day of joy That thou expect'st not, nor I looked not for.	75
Juliet	Madam, in happy time, what day is that?	
Lady Capulet	Marry my child, early next Thursday morn, The gallant, young and noble gentleman, The County Paris, at Saint Peter's Church, Shall happily make thee there a joyful bride.	80
Juliet	Now, by Saint Peter's Church, and Peter too, He shall not make me there a joyful bride. I pray you, tell my lord and father, madam, I will not marry yet, and when I do, I swear It shall be Romeo, whom you know I hate, Rather than Paris. These are news indeed!	85
Lady Capulet	Here comes your father, tell him so yourself, And see how he will take it at your hands.	
	Enter Capulet and Nurse.	
Capulet	How now? A conduit, girl? What, still in tears? Evermore show'ring? How now, wife? Have you delivered to her our decree?	90

Notes:

51 **feeling:** deeply felt

55 **Villain and he ... asunder:** Romeo is far from being a villain [From this point, Juliet picks her words to mislead her mother about her feelings for Romeo]

57 **no man ... my heart:** no man can cause me the distress he has

60 **Would:** I wish

60 **venge:** take revenge for

66 **temper:** mix something into

67 **upon receipt thereof:** when he has it

72 **careful:** caring

73 **heaviness:** sadness

74 **sorted out:** arranged

75 **nor I looked not for:** and I wasn't expecting

76 **in happy time:** how lucky

77 **Marry:** a mild oath – by Mary (Christ's mother)

86 **These are news indeed!:** what a thing to tell me

88 **at your hands:** from you

89 **conduit:** water pipe

91 **our decree:** my decision

Juliet and Capulet
Which line was being spoken when this photograph
was taken – line 94, line 102, or line 105?

These questions are about all of Act 3 Scene 5.

2 How would you advise Capulet to speak and move
when he hears that Juliet is refusing to marry Paris?

3 What does Capulet reveal about his character in this
scene?

4 What does Lady Capulet reveal about her character
in this scene?

5 How does this scene add to what we know about
the theme of the place of women in society at the
time?

Lady Capulet	Ay, sir, but she will none, she gives you thanks.
	I would the fool were married to her grave.
Capulet	Soft, take me with you, take me with you, wife.
	How, will she none? Doth she not give us thanks? 95
	Is she not proud? Doth she not count her blest,
	Unworthy as she is, that we have wrought
	So worthy a gentleman to be her bridegroom?
Juliet	Not proud you have, but thankful, that you have.
	Proud can I never be of what I hate, 100
	But thankful even for hate, that is meant love.
Capulet	How how? How how? Chopped-logic? What is this?
	"Proud", and "I thank you", and "I thank you not".
	And yet "not proud"? Mistress minion you?
	Thank me no thankings, nor, proud me no prouds, 105
	But fettle your fine joints 'gainst Thursday next,
	To go with Paris to Saint Peter's Church,
	Or I will drag thee on a hurdle thither.
	Out you green-sickness carrion, out you baggage,
	You tallow-face!
Lady Capulet	Fie, fie, what, are you mad? 110
Juliet	Good father, I beseech you on my knees,
	Hear me with patience but to speak a word.
Capulet	Hang thee young baggage, disobedient wretch!
	I tell thee what, get thee to church o' Thursday,
	Or never after look me in the face. 115
	Speak not, reply not, do not answer me.
	My fingers itch. Out on her, hilding!
Nurse	You are to blame my lord, to rate her so.
Capulet	Peace, you mumbling fool!
Lady Capulet	You are too hot. 120
Capulet	God's bread, it makes me mad!
	Day, night, hour, tide, time, work, play,
	Alone, in company, still my care hath been
	To have her matched. And having now provided
	A gentleman of noble parentage, 125
	And then to have a wretched puling fool,
	To answer, "I'll not wed, I cannot love.
	I am too young, I pray you, pardon me."
	But, if you will not wed, I'll pardon you!
	Graze where you will you shall not house with me. 130
	If you be mine, I'll give you to my friend.
	If you be not: hang, beg, starve, die in the streets.
	Trust to't, bethink you, I'll not be forsworn. *He exits.*
Juliet	O sweet my mother, cast me not away.
	Delay this marriage for a month, a week! 135

92 **she will none:** she won't do it

94 **Soft, take me with you:** hold on, explain

96 **count her:** consider herself

97 **wrought:** persuaded

99 **Not proud … thankful:** I'm not pleased, but I am grateful

101 **thankful even … meant love:** I'm grateful for what you have done out of love, but I hate the thing itself

102 **Chopped-logic:** over-clever arguments

104 **mistress minion:** spoilt little madam

106 **fettle your fine joints:** get your fussy self ready

108 **hurdle:** rough wooden frame used to drag traitors to execution

109 **Out:** used to show disgust

109 **green-sickness carrion:** bloodless corpse

109 **baggage:** a good-for nothing woman

110 **tallow-face:** face as white as candle wax

110 **fie:** used to reproach someone for unsuitable behaviour

117 **My fingers itch:** I long to slap you

117 **hilding:** a good-for nothing horse or woman

118 **rate her so:** scold her so violently

123–4 **still my care … her matched:** I've been constantly thinking about finding her a good husband

126 **puling:** whining

130 **Graze where... with me:** you can fend for yourself, I won't have you in the house

133 **be forsworn:** break my word

Juliet is rejected by her mother, lines 136–7.
Look back at the photographs from this scene (and this production) on pages 62–8. What emotions does Shakespeare give Juliet in this scene?

Lady Capulet	Talk not to me, for I'll not speak a word.
	Do as thou wilt, for I have done with thee. *She exits.*
Juliet	O God! O Nurse, how shall this be prevented?
	What say'st thou? Hast thou not a word of joy?
	Some comfort Nurse. **140**
Nurse	Faith, here it is. Romeo is banished.
	Then, since the case so stands as now it doth,
	I think it best you married with the County.
	O he's a lovely gentleman!
	Romeo's a dishclout to him. Beshrew my heart, **145**
	I think you are happy in this second match,
	For it excels your first. Or if it did not,
	Your first is dead, or 'twere as good he were,
	As living here and you no use of him.
Juliet	Speakest thou from thy heart? **150**
Nurse	And from my soul too, or else beshrew them both.
Juliet	Amen.
Nurse	What?
Juliet	Well, thou hast comforted me marvellous much.
	Go in, and tell my lady I am gone, **155**
	Having displeased my father, to Lawrence' cell,
	To make confession and to be absolved.
Nurse	Marry, I will, and this is wisely done. *She exits.*
Juliet	Ancient damnation! O most wicked fiend!
	Go, counsellor, **160**
	Thou and my bosom henceforth shall be twain.
	I'll to the Friar to know his remedy,
	If all else fail, myself have power to die. *She exits.*

143 **the County:** Paris

145 **dishclout:** dishcloth
145 **Beshrew my very heart:** honestly [literal meaning 'curse my heart']
146 **happy:** lucky
148 **'twere as good he were:** he might as well be
149 **As living ... no use of him:** he's no use to you if you can't be together

155 **my lady:** my mother
159 **Ancient damnation!:** damn you, old woman
161 **Thou and my... twain:** I won't share my thoughts with you again
162 **I'll to:** I'll go to
162 **his remedy:** his solution to the problem
163 **myself ... to die:** I'll find a way to kill myself

These questions ask you to reflect on all of Act 3.

a) How important is it for an audience to know how families controlled their children's futures to understand the events in Act 3?

b) How does Romeo change throughout the Act?

c) How are words and imagery used in Act 3 to show the power of different people's emotions?

d) How is true love contrasted with family honour in Act 3?

e) In what way are the actions of Friar Lawrence and the Nurse in Act 3 significant?

Juliet, lines 30–32
After all the terrible events of the previous scene, Juliet goes to the only person she trusts in Verona who knows her full story. What is her first problem in this scene?

Act 4 Scene 1

Enter Friar Lawrence and Paris.

Friar Lawrence	On Thursday sir? The time is very short.
Paris	My father Capulet will have it so,
	And I am nothing slow to slack his haste.
Friar Lawrence	You say you do not know the lady's mind?
	Uneven is the course, I like it not.
Paris	Immoderately she weeps for Tybalt's death,
	And therefore have I little talked of love,
	For Venus smiles not in a house of tears.
Friar Lawrence	Look sir, here comes the lady towards my cell.

Enter Juliet.

Paris	Happily met, my lady and my wife.
Juliet	That may be, sir, when I may be a wife.
Paris	That "may be" must be, love, on Thursday next.
Juliet	What "must be" shall be.
Friar Lawrence	That's a certain text.
Paris	Come you to make confession to this father?
Juliet	Are you at leisure, holy father, now,
	Or shall I come to you at evening mass?
Friar Lawrence	My leisure serves me, pensive daughter, now.
	My lord, we must entreat the time alone.
Paris	God shield I should disturb devotion.
	Juliet, on Thursday early will I rouse ye,
	Till then, adieu, and keep this holy kiss. *He exits.*
Juliet	O shut the door, and when thou hast done so
	Come weep with me, past hope, past care, past help.
Friar Lawrence	O Juliet, I already know thy grief,
	It strains me past the compass of my wits.
	I hear thou must, and nothing may prorogue it,
	On Thursday next be married to this County.
Juliet	Tell me not, Friar, that thou hear'st of this,
	Unless thou tell me how I may prevent it.
	Give me some present counsel, or behold
	'Twixt my extremes and me this bloody knife
	Shall play the umpire, I long to die,
	If what thou speak'st speak not of remedy.
Friar Lawrence	Hold daughter, I do spy a kind of hope,
	If, rather than to marry County Paris,
	Thou hast the strength of will to slay thyself.
	Then is it likely thou wilt undertake
	A thing like death, to chide away this shame.
	And if thou darest, I'll give thee remedy.

Line numbers: 5, 10, 15, 20, 25, 30, 35

3 **I am ... his haste:** I've no reason to want to slow him down

4 **the lady's mind:** what Juliet thinks of it

5 **Uneven is the course:** this is not the normal way to do this

8 **Venus smiles not:** the goddess of love is not happy

10 **Happily:** fortunately

13 **a certain text:** a saying – that's right

17 **My leisure serves me:** I'm free

17 **pensive:** double meaning: thoughtful; sad

17 **daughter:** he is her spiritual father

18 **entreat the time alone:** need to be alone

19 **shield:** forbid

20 **rouse:** wake

23 **care:** spiritual help

25 **It strains me ... my wits:** I can't think of a solution

26 **prorogue:** postpone

30 **present counsel:** advice, now

31 **'Twixt:** between

31 **my extremes:** my appalling situation

32 **shall play the umpire:** will provide the solution

33 **speak not of remedy:** doesn't give an answer

34 **Hold:** wait

38 **A thing like death:** something similar to death

38 **chide away:** drive away

38 **this shame:** [marrying Paris]

Friar Lawrence, about lines 46–8
Why might the director of this production have chosen to have Friar Lawrence mix the potion rather than just pick up a vial ready mixed? Does it suggest anything about the power of the potion?

These questions are about all of Act 4 Scene 1.

1 Paris is determined to marry Juliet, even though she is clearly upset and hasn't accepted him. How does this add to the theme of love in the play?

2 When Juliet talks to Friar Lawrence, how do the words and imagery she uses show the audience how desperate she is to find a way out of the situation she finds herself in?

3 How would you tell the actor playing Friar Lawrence to speak and move, to show that he is in control of the situation? Think about the way he tells Juliet his plan at the end of the scene.

4 How do Friar Lawrence's actions in this scene emphasise that his behaviour is not that normally expected of a religious friar? Think about the things he says to Paris at the start of the scene, and his plan to deceive the Capulet family.

Juliet	O bid me leap, rather than marry Paris,	**40**
	From off the battlements of any tower,	
	Or bid me go into a new-made grave	
	And I will do it without fear or doubt,	
	To live an unstained wife to my sweet love.	

44 unstained: faithful

Friar Lawrence	Hold then. Go home, be merry, give consent	**45**
	To marry Paris. Wednesday is tomorrow,	
	Tomorrow night look that thou lie alone.	
	Take thou this vial, being then in bed,	
	And this distilling liquor drink thou off,	
	When presently through all thy veins shall run	**50**
	A cold and drowsy humour. For no pulse	
	No warmth, no breath, shall testify thou livest.	
	Each part, deprived of supple government,	
	Shall stiff and stark and cold appear like death,	
	And in this borrowed likeness of shrunk death	**55**
	Thou shalt continue two and forty hours,	
	And then awake as from a pleasant sleep.	
	Now when the bridegroom in the morning comes	
	To rouse thee from thy bed, there art thou dead.	
	Then, as the manner of our country is,	**60**
	In thy best robes uncovered on the bier,	
	Thou shalt be borne to that same ancient vault	
	Where all the kindred of the Capulets lie.	
	In the mean time, against thou shalt awake,	
	Shall Romeo by my letters know our drift,	**65**
	And hither shall he come, and he and I	
	Will watch thy waking, and that very night	
	Shall Romeo bear thee hence to Mantua.	

47 look that thou lie: make sure you sleep
48 vial: very small bottle
49 distilling liquor: strong liquid
49 drink thou off: drink up completely
50 When presently: at once
51 A cold … humour: a feeling of cold and sleepiness
51–2 For no pulse … thou livest: your pulse will seem to stop
53 supple government: the power to move
55 borrowed likeness: imitation
60 as the manner of our country is: in the way we do things here
61 bier: the moveable stand a body is carried to the grave on
62 vault: tomb
64 against thou shalt wake: in preparation for when you wake
65 our drift: what we have planned
68 bear thee hence: take you away

Juliet	Give me, give me! O, tell not me of fear!	
Friar Lawrence	Hold, get you gone, be strong and prosperous	**70**
	In this resolve. I'll send a friar with speed	
	To Mantua with my letters to thy lord.	
Juliet	Love give me strength and strength shall help afford.	
	Farewell, dear father.	*They exit.*

70 prosperous: lucky

Act 4 Scene 2

Enter Capulet, Lady Capulet, Nurse, and Servants.

Capulet	So many guests invite as here are writ. *Exit a Servant.*	
	What, is my daughter gone to Friar Lawrence?	
Nurse	Ay forsooth.	
Capulet	Well, he may chance to do some good on her.	
	A peevish self-willed harlotry it is. *Enter Juliet.*	**5**
	How now, my headstrong, where have you been gadding?	
Juliet	Where I have learnt me to repent the sin	

1 So many … are writ: here's a list of guests to invite
3 Ay forsooth: yes, indeed
5 A peevish … it is: she's a moody, stubborn little madam
6 my headstrong: my stubborn child
6 gadding: wandering off to

These questions are about all of Act 4 Scene 2.

1 How do the words Capulet uses to describe Juliet show his feelings about her?

2 How would you advise the actor playing Capulet to move and speak, to show the audience the way he feels in this scene?

3 How does the treatment of Juliet in this scene develop the theme of the place of women in society?

4 Do Juliet's actions in this scene show her growing maturity?

Juliet (Act 4 Scene 2, line 9) is looking at her father and mother, who are on the opposite side of the stage.
At this moment in this production, Juliet was isolated on the Globe's large stage. What effect might this have on the audience?

	Of disobedient opposition,	
	And beg your pardon. Pardon, I beseech you,	
	Henceforward I am ever ruled by you.	10
Capulet	Send for the County, go tell him of this.	
	I'll have this knot knit up tomorrow morning.	
Juliet	Nurse, will you go with me into my closet,	
	To help me sort such needful ornaments	
	As you think fit to furnish me tomorrow?	15
Lady Capulet	No, not till Thursday; there is time enough.	
Capulet	Go, Nurse, go with her. We'll to church tomorrow.	

Exit Juliet and Nurse.

	And all things shall be well, I warrant thee, wife:	
	Go thou to Juliet, help to deck up her;	
	I'll not to bed tonight; let me alone,	20
	My heart is wondrous light.	*Exit all.*

10 Henceforward: from now on
10 I am ever ruled by: I will always obey
12 this knot: the marriage
13 closet: private room
14 sort: choose
14 needful: necessary
15 fit to furnish me: suitable to wear
18 warrant: promise

19 deck up her: choose what she'll wear
20 let me alone: let me deal with it

Act 4 Scene 3

Enter Juliet and Nurse, a bed with curtains on stage.

Juliet	Ay, those attires are best. But gentle nurse	
	I pray thee leave me to myself tonight.	

Enter Lady Capulet.

Lady Capulet	What, are you busy, ho? Need you my help?	
Juliet	So please you, let me now be left alone,	
	And let the Nurse this night sit up with you,	5
	For I am sure you have your hands full all	
	In this so sudden business.	
Lady Capulet	Good night.	
	Get thee to bed and rest for thou hast need.	

Exit Lady Capulet and Nurse.

Juliet	Farewell. God knows when we shall meet again.	
	Come vial. What if this mixture do not work at all?	10
	Shall I be married then tomorrow morning?	

Taking out a dagger.

	No, no, this shall forbid it. Lie thou there.	
	What if it be a poison, which the Friar	
	Subtly hath ministered to have me dead,	
	Lest in this marriage he should be dishonoured,	15
	Because he married me before to Romeo?	
	How, if when I am laid into the tomb,	
	I wake before the time that Romeo	
	Come to redeem me? There's a fearful point.	
	Shall I not, then, be stifled in the vault,	20
	And there die strangled ere my Romeo comes?	

1 attires: clothes

10 vial: very small bottle

14 Subtly hath ministered: has cunningly given me
15 Lest in ... be dishonoured: in case he's found out and disgraced
17 How, if: what if
19 redeem: save, rescue
20 stifled: suffocated
21 strangled: choked, dead from lack of air
21 ere: before

These questions are about all of Act 4 Scene 3.

1   How do the words and imagery used by Juliet show how frightened she is about the plan for her to be buried in the family vault?

2   How do Juliet's fears about the drug and her worries about waking in the dark tomb show the power that love can exert over a person?

3   How do Juliet's actions show her awareness of the consequences of marrying Paris?

The Nurse discovers Juliet, Act 4 Scene 5, line 8.
How far is the Nurse panicking at this point?

Or if I live, is it not very like
So early waking, what with loathsome smells,
And shrieks like mandrakes torn out of the earth,
That living mortals, hearing them, run mad — **25**
O if I wake, shall I not be distraught,
Environèd with all these hideous fears.
And in this rage, with some great kinsman's bone,
As with a club, dash out my desp'rate brains?
O look, methinks I see my cousin's ghost **30**
Seeking out Romeo that did spit his body
Upon a rapier's point. Stay, Tybalt, stay!
Romeo, Romeo, Romeo, here's drink. I drink to thee!

She drinks, and falls on the bed, within the curtains.

22	**is it not like:** isn't it likely
24	**mandrakes:** plants said to scream when pulled up, causing those who heard the screams to go mad and die
27	**Environèd with:** surrounded by
28	**rage:** madness
31	**spit:** skewer
32	**Stay!:** stop!

Act 4 Scene 4

Enter Capulet, Lady Capulet and Nurse.

Capulet
Come, stir, stir, stir! The second cock hath crowed,
The curfew-bell hath rung, 'tis three o'clock.

Exit Lady Capulet and Nurse. Music offstage.

The County will be here with music straight.
Nurse! Wife! What ho? What, Nurse, I say!
Enter Nurse. Go waken Juliet, go and trim her up. **5**
I'll go and chat with Paris. Hie, make haste,
Make haste, the bridegroom he is come already.
Make haste I say. *They exit.*

2	**curfew-bell:** bell rung in the early morning when the watchmen went off duty and the city gates were unlocked
3	**straight:** any minute
5	**trim her up:** get her dressed

Act 4 Scene 5

The Nurse goes to the bed.

Nurse
Mistress, what mistress? Juliet?
Why lamb, why lady? Fie, you slugabed!
Why love I say? Madam? Sweetheart? Why bride?
— Marry, and amen, how sound is she asleep?
I needs must wake her. — Madam, madam, madam! **5**

She opens the bed curtains.

What, dressed, and in your clothes, and down again?
I must needs wake you. Lady, lady, lady?
Alas, alas! Help, help! My lady's dead!
O weraday, that ever I was born!
Some aqua vitae, ho! My lord! My lady! **10**

Enter Lady Capulet.

Lady Capulet What noise is here?

Nurse O lamentable day!

What's just happened
- Juliet has taken the drug Friar Lawrence gave her.
- The drug makes it seem she is dead.
- The whole household is expecting a wedding.

5	**I must needs:** I really have to
6	**dressed ... down again:** dressed, and then gone back to sleep in your clothes
9	**weraday:** alas
10	**aqua vitae:** brandy

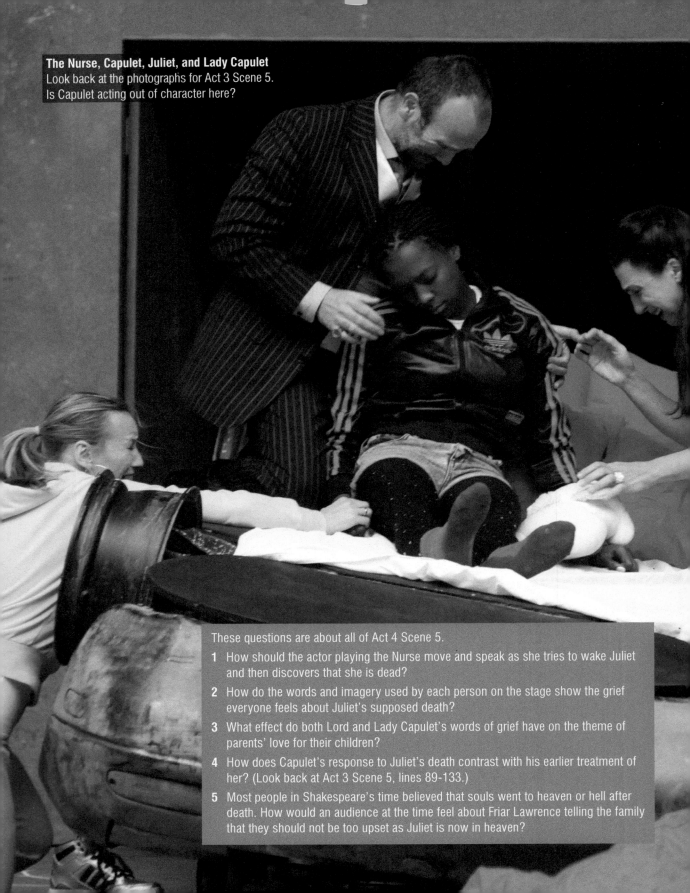

The Nurse, Capulet, Juliet, and Lady Capulet
Look back at the photographs for Act 3 Scene 5.
Is Capulet acting out of character here?

These questions are about all of Act 4 Scene 5.

1 How should the actor playing the Nurse move and speak as she tries to wake Juliet and then discovers that she is dead?

2 How do the words and imagery used by each person on the stage show the grief everyone feels about Juliet's supposed death?

3 What effect do both Lord and Lady Capulet's words of grief have on the theme of parents' love for their children?

4 How does Capulet's response to Juliet's death contrast with his earlier treatment of her? (Look back at Act 3 Scene 5, lines 89-133.)

5 Most people in Shakespeare's time believed that souls went to heaven or hell after death. How would an audience at the time feel about Friar Lawrence telling the family that they should not be too upset as Juliet is now in heaven?

Lady Capulet	What is the matter?		
Nurse	Look, look. O heavy day!		**12 heavy:** unhappy
Lady Capulet	O me, O me, my child, my only life.		**13 my only life:** the only child I have
	Revive, look up, or I will die with thee!		
	Help, help! Call help! *Enter Capulet.*	15	

Capulet   For shame, bring Juliet forth, her lord is come.

Nurse   She's dead. Deceased. She's dead. Alack the day!

Lady Capulet   Alack the day, she's dead, she's dead, she's dead!

Capulet   Ha! Let me see her. Out, alas, she's cold:
Her blood is settled and her joints are stiff.   20

20 is settled: isn't moving round her body

Nurse   O lamentable day!

Lady Capulet   O woeful time!

Capulet   Death, that hath ta'en her hence to make me wail,
Ties up my tongue, and will not let me speak.

22 ta'en her hence: taken her away

Enter Friar Lawrence and County Paris with Musicians.

Friar Lawrence   Come, is the bride ready to go to church?

Capulet   Ready to go, but never to return.   25
O son, the night before thy wedding day
Hath Death lain with thy wife. There she lies,
Death is my son-in-law, Death is my heir.

27 lain with: slept with

Paris   Have I thought long to see this morning's face,
And doth it give me such a sight as this?   30

29 Have I thought ... face: I've waited so impatiently for this morning

Lady Capulet   Accursed, unhappy, wretched, hateful day!
But one, poor one, one poor and loving child,
But one thing to rejoice and solace in,
And cruel Death hath catched it from my sight!

33 solace in: take comfort from
34 hath catched it: has snatched this child

Nurse   O woe! O woeful, woeful, woeful day!   35
Most lamentable day, most woeful day,
That ever, ever, I did yet behold!
O day, O day, O day, O hateful day,
Never was seen so black a day as this.
O woeful day, O woeful day!   40

Paris   Beguiled, divorcèd, wrongèd, spited, slain!
Most detestable Death, by thee beguiled,
By cruel, cruel thee quite overthrown.
O love, O life! Not life, but love in death!

41 Beguiled: cheated

Capulet   Despised, distressèd, hated, martyred, killed!   45
Uncomfortable time, why cam'st thou now
To murder, murder our solemnity?
O child, O child! My soul and not my child,
Dead art thou! Alack my child is dead,
And with my child, my joys are burièd.   50

46 Uncomfortable: without comfort
47 murder our solemnity: kill her and so kill our celebration

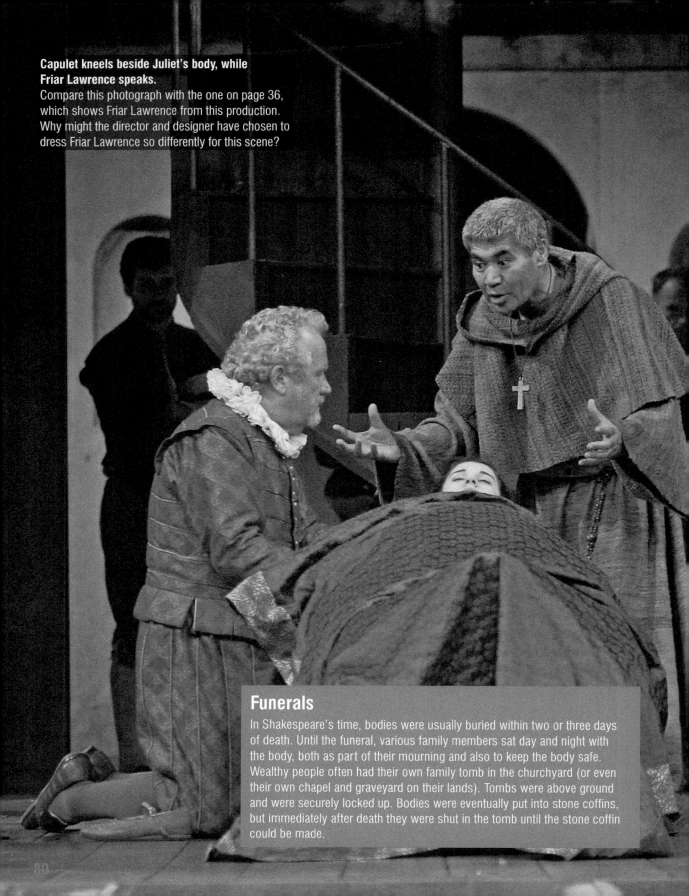

Capulet kneels beside Juliet's body, while Friar Lawrence speaks.
Compare this photograph with the one on page 36, which shows Friar Lawrence from this production. Why might the director and designer have chosen to dress Friar Lawrence so differently for this scene?

Funerals

In Shakespeare's time, bodies were usually buried within two or three days of death. Until the funeral, various family members sat day and night with the body, both as part of their mourning and also to keep the body safe. Wealthy people often had their own family tomb in the churchyard (or even their own chapel and graveyard on their lands). Tombs were above ground and were securely locked up. Bodies were eventually put into stone coffins, but immediately after death they were shut in the tomb until the stone coffin could be made.

Friar Lawrence Peace, ho, for shame! Confusion's cure lives not
In these confusions. Heaven and yourself
Had part in this fair maid, now heaven hath all,
And all the better is it for the maid.
Sir, go you in, and madam, go with him, 55
And go Sir Paris, every one prepare
To follow this fair corse unto her grave.
The heavens do lour upon you for some ill,
Move them no more by crossing their high will. 60

*Exit Capulet, Lady Capulet, Paris, and Friar
Lawrence, each putting rosemary on the body,
shutting the bed curtains. They are followed by
the Nurse and the Musicians.*

51–2 **Confusion's cure ... these confusions:** we can't sort things out until we all calm down
53 **Had part in:** shared
57 **corse:** corpse
59 **lour:** frown

These questions ask you to reflect on all of Act 4.

a) How are words and imagery used in Act 4 to emphasise extreme emotions such as fear and grief?

b) How should Lord and Lady Capulet and the Nurse behave as the different events occur in Act 4?

c) How important is it to understand the relationship between parents and their children in Shakespeare's time when watching events unfold in Act 4?

d) How is the theme of true love contrasted with arranged marriage through the events of Act 4?

e) How does Juliet develop as a person during Act 4?

Romeo

Look at his expression and his body language. Was this photograph taken before or after he hears the news from Balthasar?

1 How does Romeo's use of language help to show his state of mind?

2 If you were directing a production of the play, how would you want the actor playing Romeo to move and speak as he hears Balthasar's news about Juliet?

Act 5 Scene 1

Enter Romeo.

Romeo	If I may trust the flattering truth of sleep, My dreams presage some joyful news at hand. I dreamt my lady came and found me dead And breathed such life with kisses in my lips, That I revived and was an emperor. 5

Enter Balthasar, Romeo's servant, in riding boots.

	News from Verona. How now Balthasar? Dost thou not bring me letters from the Friar? How doth my lady? Is my father well? How doth my lady Juliet? That I ask again, For nothing can be ill, if she be well. 10
Balthasar	Then she is well, and nothing can be ill. Her body sleeps in Capel's monument, And her immortal part with angels lives. O pardon me for bringing these ill news.
Romeo	Is it even so? Then I deny you, stars. — 15 Get me ink and paper, I will hence tonight.
Balthasar	I do beseech you, sir, have patience. Your looks are pale and wild, and do import Some misadventure.
Romeo	Tush, thou art deceived. Leave me, and do the thing I bid thee do. 20 Hast thou no letters to me from the Friar?
Balthasar	No, my good lord.
Romeo	No matter. Get thee gone, I'll be with thee straight. *Exit Balthasar.* Well, Juliet, I will lie with thee tonight. Let's see for means. O mischief, thou art swift 25 To enter in the thoughts of desperate men. I do remember an apothecary, And hereabouts 'a dwells, which late I noted In tattered weeds, with overwhelming brows, Sharp misery had worn him to the bones. 30 Noting this penury, to myself I said, "An if a man did need a poison now, Here lives a caitiff wretch would sell it him." What ho! Apothecary! *[Enter Apothecary.]*
Apothecary	Who calls so loud?
Romeo	Come hither man. I see that thou art poor, 35 Hold, there is forty ducats, let me have A dram of poison, such soon-speeding gear

What's just happened

- Romeo is in exile.
- Everyone in Verona thinks Juliet is dead.
- Romeo has heard nothing from Friar Lawrence.

1 **the flattering truth of sleep:** what my dreams tell me
2 **presage:** predict
12 **Capel's monument:** the Capulet tomb
13 **immortal part:** soul
15 **Is it even so?:** so that's what's happened
15 **I deny you, stars:** I won't accept the influence of the stars on events
18–9 **do import … misadventure:** nothing good can come of acting now
19 **Tush:** don't be foolish
25 **Let's see for means:** how can I do it
25 **mischief:** evil
27 **apothecary:** someone who prepared and sold medicines
28 **hereabouts 'a dwells:** he lives around here
28 **which late I noted:** I saw him recently
29 **tattered weeds:** ragged clothes
29 **overwhelming brows:** overgrown, uncared for eyebrows
31 **penury:** obvious lack of money
33 **a caitiff wretch:** a poor man desperate enough
35 **hither:** here
36 **ducats:** gold coins
37 **dram:** a small quantity
37 **soon-speeding gear:** stuff that works fast

A

B

C

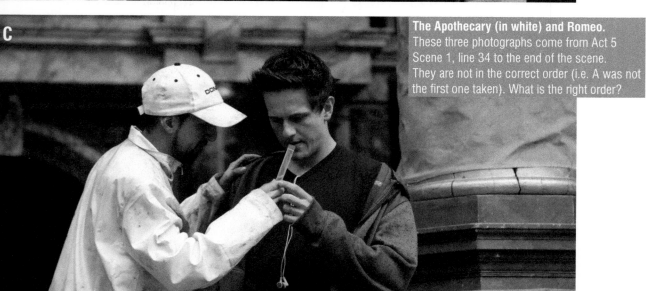

The Apothecary (in white) and Romeo.
These three photographs come from Act 5
Scene 1, line 34 to the end of the scene.
They are not in the correct order (i.e. A was not
the first one taken). What is the right order?

As will disperse itself through all the veins,
That the life-weary taker may fall dead.

Apothecary	Such mortal drugs I have, but Mantua's law	**40**
	Is death to any he that utters them.	
Romeo	Art thou so bare and full of wretchedness,	
	And fear'st to die? Famine is in thy cheeks,	
	The world is not thy friend, nor the world's law.	
	The world affords no law to make thee rich.	**45**
	Then be not poor, but break it, and take this.	
Apothecary	My poverty, but not my will, consents.	
Romeo	I pay thy poverty, and not thy will.	
Apothecary	Put this in any liquid thing you will	
	And drink it off, and if you had the strength	**50**
	Of twenty men, it would dispatch you straight.	
Romeo	There is thy gold, worse poison to men's souls,	
	Doing more murder in this loathsome world	
	Than these poor compounds that thou mayst not sell.	
	Come, cordial and not poison, go with me	**55**
	To Juliet's grave, for there must I use thee. *They exit.*	

Glossary

40 **mortal:** deadly
41 **he that utters:** man that sells
42 **bare:** poor
43 **And fear'st:** yet still fear
45 **affords:** gives you
47 **My poverty … consents:** poverty forces me to take it, but I don't want to
51 **dispatch you straight:** kill you instantly
54 **poor compounds:** wretched mixtures
55 **cordial:** medicine to make you well

Act 5 Scene 2

Enter Friar John and Friar Lawrence by different doors.

Friar John	Holy Franciscan friar, brother, ho!	
Friar Lawrence	This same should be the voice of Friar John.	
	Welcome from Mantua, what says Romeo?	
	Or, if his mind be writ, give me his letter.	
Friar John	Going to find a barefoot brother out,	**5**
	One of our order, to associate me,	
	Here in this city visiting the sick,	
	And finding him, the searchers of the town	
	Suspecting that we both were in a house	
	Where the infectious pestilence did reign,	**10**
	Sealed up the doors, and would not let us forth,	
	So that my speed to Mantua there was stayed.	
Friar Lawrence	Who bare my letter then to Romeo?	
Friar John	I could not send it — here it is again.	
Friar Lawrence	Unhappy fortune! By my brotherhood,	**15**
	The letter was not nice but full of charge,	
	Of dear import, and the neglecting it	
	May do much danger. Friar John, go hence,	
	Get me an iron crow and bring it straight	
	Unto my cell.	**20**
Friar John	Brother, I'll go and bring it thee. *He exits.*	

Glossary

4 **if his mind be writ:** if he's written to me
5 **barefoot brother:** Franciscan friar
6 **associate me:** travel with me [friars had to travel in pairs]
8 **searchers:** officials who viewed dead bodies to find the cause of death
10 **pestilence:** plague
11 **forth:** out
12 **my speed … stayed:** I couldn't go to Mantua
13 **bare:** took
16 **nice:** trivial
16 **charge:** serious information
17 **Of dear import:** vitally important
19 **an iron crow:** a crow-bar
19 **straight:** at once

1 How do the words and imagery used by Romeo show his feeling when he sees what he thinks is Juliet's dead body?

Romeo with (he thinks) the dead body of Juliet. Does this photograph best fit lines 10–11, line 18, or line 19?

Friar Lawrence	Now must I to the monument alone,		
	Within this three hours will fair Juliet wake,		
	She will beshrew me much that Romeo		
	Hath had no notice of these accidents.	**25**	
	But I will write again to Mantua,		
	And keep her at my cell till Romeo come.		
	Poor living corse, closed in a dead man's tomb!	*He exits.*	

22 the monument: the Capulet tomb

24 beshrew me much: abuse me

25 these accidents: what's happened

28 corse: corpse

Act 5 Scene 3

Juliet's body is on stage. Enter Romeo.

Romeo	O my love, my wife,		
	Death that hath sucked the honey of thy breath,		
	Hath had no power yet upon thy beauty.		
	Thou art not conquered. Ah, dear Juliet,		
	Why art thou yet so fair? Shall I believe	**5**	
	That unsubstantial death is amorous,		
	And that the lean abhorrèd monster keeps		
	Thee here in dark to be his paramour?		
	For fear of that, I still will stay with thee,		
	And never from this palace of dim night	**10**	
	Depart again. Here, here will I remain		
	With worms that are thy chamber-maids. O here		
	Will I set up my everlasting rest		
	And shake the yoke of inauspicious stars		
	From this world-wearied flesh. Eyes, look your last.	**15**	
	Arms, take your last embrace. And lips, O you		
	The doors of breath, seal with a righteous kiss		
	A dateless bargain to engrossing Death. *[Kisses her.]*		
	Come bitter conduct, come unsavoury guide,		
	Thou desperate pilot, now at once run on	**20**	
	The dashing rocks thy sea-sick weary bark.		
	Here's to my love. *[He drinks.]* O true apothecary,		
	Thy drugs are quick. Thus with a kiss I die. *[He dies.]*		

Enter Friar Lawrence, with a lantern.

5 yet: still

6–8 unsubstantial ... his paramour: skeleton-like Death loves you and keeps you here to be his lover

9 still: always

14 shake the yoke ... stars: throw off my unlucky fate

18 A dateless ... Death: an everlasting contract with Death who gets everything

19 conduct: guide

20 pilot: navigator that guides a ship into harbour

21 sea-sick weary bark: ship, sick of sailing [Romeo's body]

22 true: honest, truthful

Friar Lawrence	Romeo!		
	Romeo! O, pale! Ah, what an unkind hour	**25**	
	Is guilty of this lamentable chance? *[Juliet wakes.]*		
	The lady stirs.		
Juliet	O comfortable Friar, where is my lord?		
	I do remember well where I should be,		
	And there I am. Where is my Romeo?	**30**	
Friar Lawrence	I hear some noise lady. Come from that nest		
	Of death, contagion, and unnatural sleep.		
	Thy husband in thy bosom there lies dead,		
	Stay not to question, for the Watch is coming.		

25 unkind hour: cruel circumstance

26 this lamentable chance: tragic accident

28 comfortable: reassuring

32 contagion: infectious disease

Juliet kisses the dead Romeo (line 40).

2 How does Juliet's final speech (lines 37–45) emphasise the tragedy that has just occurred?

	Come, go, good Juliet, I dare no longer stay.	35
Juliet	Go, get thee hence, for I will not away.	

Exit Friar Lawrence.

What's here? A cup closed in my true love's hand?
Poison, I see, hath been his timeless end.
O churl, drunk all? And left no friendly drop
To help me after? I will kiss thy lips, **40**
Haply some poison yet doth hang on them,
To make me die with a restorative. *[Kisses him.]*
Thy lips are warm. *[Noise of people talking offstage.]*
Yea, noise? Then I'll be brief. O happy dagger!

Taking Romeo's dagger.

This is thy sheath, there rust, and let me die. **45**

She stabs herself and falls.

Enter the Prince, with attendants, and a
Watchman with Friar Lawrence.

Prince	What calls our person from our morning's rest?	

Enter Capulet and Lady Capulet.

Capulet	What should it be, that they so shriek abroad?	
First Watchman	Sovereign, here lies Romeo dead,	
	And Juliet, dead before, warm and new killed.	
	Here is a friar —	50
Capulet	O heavens! O wife, look how our daughter bleeds!	

Enter Montague.

Prince	Come Montague, for thou art early up	
	To see thy son and heir now early down.	
Montague	Alas, my liege, my wife is dead tonight,	
	What further woe conspires against mine age?	55
Prince	Look, and thou shalt see.	
	Seal up the mouth of outrage for a while.	
Friar Lawrence	Romeo, there dead, was husband to that Juliet,	
	And she, there dead, that's Romeo's faithful wife.	
	I married them, and their stol'n marriage-day	60
	Was Tybalt's doomsday, whose untimely death	
	Banished the new-made bridegroom from this city.	
Prince	Where's Romeo's man? What can he say to this?	
Balthasar	I brought my master news of Juliet's death.	
	This letter he early bid me give his father.	65
Prince	Give me the letter, I will look on it.	
	This letter doth make good the Friar's words,	
	Their course of love, the tidings of her death.	
	And here he writes that he did buy a poison	

38 hath been his timeless end: has killed him

39 churl: bad-mannered person

40 To help me after: for me to take to follow you [into death]

41 Haply: perhaps

42 restorative: double meaning: brings back to life; takes her to be with him

44 brief: quick

44 happy: found at just the right moment

47 What should … abroad?: what is everyone yelling about?

53 early down: dead before you were up

54 is dead tonight: died in the night

57 Seal up the mouth of outrage: quieten your grief

60 stol'n: secret

61 Tybalt's doomsday: the day Tybalt died

65 early: early the next morning

67 make good: confirm

Capulet (left) and Montague (right), lines 75–6
The bodies of Juliet and Romeo are in the background.
This photograph sums up the end of the story of the
play, and the resolution of some of its themes.
Pick two other photographs from this book that could go
with this one to sum up the play.

	Of a poor 'pothecary, and therewithal	70
	Came to this vault to die, and lie with Juliet.	
	Where be these enemies? Capulet, Montague?	
	See what a scourge is laid upon your hate	
	That heaven finds means to kill your joys with love.	

Capulet   O brother Montague, give me thy hand,   **75**
This is my daughter's jointure, for no more
Can I demand.

Montague   But I can give thee more.
For I will raise her statue in pure gold,
That while Verona by that name is known,
There shall no figure at such rate be set   **80**
As that of true and faithful Juliet.

Capulet   As rich shall Romeo's by his lady's lie,
Poor sacrifices of our enmity.

Prince   A glooming peace this morning with it brings,
The sun, for sorrow, will not show his head.   **85**
Go hence, to have more talk of these sad things,
Some shall be pardoned, and some punishèd.
For never was a story of more woe
Than this of Juliet, and her Romeo.   *They all exit.*

70 therewithal: with it [the poison]

73 scourge: punishment
74 your joys: your children

76 jointure: payment made to the bridegroom's family by the bride's family on marriage

80 There shall no figure ... be set: no one will be seen as more important
83 Romeo's: a statue to Romeo
83 Poor sacrifices to our emnity: both victims of our hatred
84 glooming: dark, clouded

These questions are about all of Act 5 Scene 3.

1 If you were directing a performance of the play, how would you advise the actor playing Juliet to move and speak as she awakes, discovers Romeo is dead, and then takes her own life?

2 In Shakespeare's time, most wealthy families had their own large tomb where family members were buried. How important is it that an audience understands this when watching the last scene of the play?

3 How does this scene bring the themes of fate and the battle between the families to a conclusion?

4 How does Prince Escalus demonstrate his good sense and leadership in this final scene?

These questions ask you to reflect on all of Act 5.

a) How are words and imagery used to make the feelings of anxiety and despair clear in Act 5?

b) How should the actors playing Romeo and Juliet change the way they move and speak as the events of Act 5 happen?

c) How does Act 5 show that fate has worked throughout the play to prove the Chorus's words at the start to be true?

d) How have both Romeo and Juliet shown that their love for each other is true as the events of Act 5 take place?

How to do well in assessment

Most importantly, you should aim to enjoy the Shakespeare play that you are reading, and start to think about why Shakespeare makes the characters act as they do and what the main themes of the story are. You should also begin to consider the language that Shakespeare uses. This is also a great start for studying Shakespeare at GCSE.

There are a series of skills that will help you in any assessment of your understanding of a Shakespeare play. They are:

● Read, understand and respond to the play clearly. Comment on the characters' behaviour and motivations, using evidence from the text.

In other words, you need to show that you know the play and can answer the question that you have been given.

● Analyse the language, form and structure that Shakespeare uses. Show your understanding of Shakespeare's techniques by explaining their effects. Use subject terminology.

Here, you show that you understand how the play has been written by commenting on the words and techniques that Shakespeare uses. Also, you should demonstrate that you understand and can use appropriate technical language.

● Show understanding of the relationship between the play and the context in which it was written.

You must show that you understand the connections between the text and the time that it was written. This could be historical events, like the Gunpowder Plot, but also people's social and cultural beliefs of the time – such as a belief in witches - and how these affect the way that the characters think and behave.

● Use a range of vocabulary and sentence structures for clarity, purpose and effect, with accurate spelling and punctuation.

This means that your work should be clear, organised and well-written. You are not expected to have perfect spelling, but you should spell key words and character names correctly and use correct grammar.

Advice for answering questions

Remember the skills explained above. You will usually not have to show every single skill in every answer that you write. For example, extract questions usually require you to cover the first two skills – commenting on characters' behaviour and looking at how the play has been written. Remember that there is not one perfect answer to any question. Consider how you feel about the characters' actions. It is perfectly acceptable to use phrases such as, 'I think,' 'I feel that' and 'In my opinion' when answering. The most thoughtful responses often show originality, but remember to support your points with sensible argument and evidence from *Romeo and Juliet*.

1 **Read Act 1 Scene 1 lines 70–95 (page 11). What does this extract show about Romeo's state of mind at this point in the play?**

Considering character

- Think about what Romeo says and how he behaves in this extract. Make a list of words to describe his behaviour, for example, *lovesick, depressed, confused*.
- Under each of the aspects that you've listed, find a short quote as evidence of Romeo's behaviour. For example: confused – '*O brawling love, O loving hate.*'
- Now build on your ideas by explaining what an audience might think about Romeo from this behaviour. Use the glossary on the right of each page to help you but remember that the best answers include a student's own ideas.

For example:

I think that Romeo seems both confused and depressed here. He talks to Benvolio about '*brawling love*' and '*loving hate.*' This suggests that love is not straightforward and it has mixed Romeo's feelings up.

Considering language and technique

To develop the skill of analysing Shakespeare's language and technique, now look back at each quote you have selected and try to say something about particular word choices and the effect that they have on you. For example:

Romeo uses contradictory ideas as, '*brawling*' which suggests fighting and hate, and seems a strange word to link with '*love*'. The words, '*loving hate*' are also opposing and emphasise Romeo's confusion. He thinks that he loves Rosaline, but her lack of interest in him has made him feel insecure and muddled.

2 **Read Act 3 Scene 5 line 90 from, 'How now, wife' to line 117 (pages 65–67). How does Shakespeare present the conflict between Juliet and her parents in this scene?**

Considering characters' behaviour

- Make three lists, one each for Juliet, Capulet and Lady Capulet, noting their thoughts and feelings. For example, Capulet: *threatening, insulting*. Juliet: *desperate, frightened*. Decide which characters behave similarly or differently to each other.
- Find evidence from the text to back up your ideas.
- Explain your ideas by showing what you think each quote could reveal about the characters and how this creates conflict in the scene. For example:

Shakespeare creates conflict in this scene through Juliet's refusal to marry Paris and her parents' angry responses. Lady Capulet calls her daughter, '*fool*' and says that she wishes that Juliet, '*were married to her grave*'. This is extremely harsh, as she seems to be wishing that Juliet should die for disobeying them. There is also heavy irony here, because Juliet will die by the play's end as a result of marrying someone her parents would not have accepted as a husband for her.

Considering language and technique

Comment on Shakespeare's word choices for these characters, and look at how they speak. Capulet asks a lot of questions, suggesting he cannot believe Juliet is refusing to obey him. He also uses verbs which suggest violence and anger. For example:

Capulet is stunned when told of Juliet's disobedience. He asks, '*How, will she none?*' then, '*Doth she not give us thanks?*' and '*Doth she not count her blest,*' showing his disbelief and shock. His repetition of the phrase, '*doth she not*', underlines this. He uses dramatic verbs, such as, '*drag*' and '*Hang*' which suggest violence and further emphasise the conflict in this scene.

Considering context

Consider how the characters' behaviour or language could be affected by the beliefs and expected behaviour of the time. For example:

Daughters were expected to obey their parents at the time. Most fathers chose their daughter's husbands, which is why Capulet expects Juliet to agree to marry Paris. He is shocked by her refusal, calling her '*Mistress minion*' – an insolent, disobedient girl.

> 3 **How does Shakespeare present the relationship between Juliet and the Nurse at different points in the play?**

- Consider the relationship at the start of the play. For example: *affectionate*, *trusting*. List character traits that might affect it. For example: Juliet: *impatient*. Nurse: *fussy*. Does it change as the play goes on? If so, how?

- List four or five scenes that show different aspects of the relationship. For example: Act 1 Scene 3 shows how long they have been close, Act 2 Scene 5 shows the Nurse teasing (but irritating) Juliet.

- Find evidence from each scene to support your views about the relationship. For example: the Nurse irritates Juliet in Act 2 Scene 5 when she claims to have no breath to give Romeo's message. Juliet snaps, '*How art though out of breath, when thou hast breath/To say to me that thou art out of breath?*'

- Consider whether their relationship helps us to understand any of the main themes of the play. For example: friendship, parents, youth and age.

Considering language and technique

Chose one scene from your list. Consider the language Juliet and the Nurse use to speak to and about each other. For example, in Act 3 Scene 5, Juliet wants support but the Nurse advises her to marry '*the County*' and calls Paris '*lovely*'. What does this (and Juliet's reaction to it) shows about the relationship at this point of the play?

Considering context

Could the relationship be affected by beliefs of the time? For example, upper class families usually had nurses, who spent more time with children than their parents. The Nurse in the play reflects this, and is far closer to Juliet than Lady Capulet.

Putting your ideas together

Shakespeare shows the relationship between Juliet and the Nurse as close for much of the play. In Act 1 Scene 3, she claims she can, '*tell her age unto an hour*' and tells a long story about Juliet falling when young. Juliet tells the Nurse to, '*stint thou*' (be quiet), showing she can speak her true feelings to her.

Points to remember

You should:
- answer the question, not spend ages retelling the story
- use short, focused quotes
- explain techniques, not just find them.

Practice questions

1 **Read Act 3 Scene 1, lines 53-81 (pages 49–51). How does Shakespeare create mood and atmosphere in this scene?**

Tybalt	I am for you. *[Drawing his sword.]*	
Romeo	Gentle Mercutio, put thy rapier up.	
Mercutio	Come sir, your *passado*. *[They fight.]*	55
Romeo	Draw, Benvolio; beat down their weapons.	
	Gentlemen, for shame, forbear this outrage!	
	Tybalt, Mercutio, the Prince expressly hath	
	Forbidden bandying in Verona streets:	
	Hold, Tybalt! Good Mercutio!	60
	During the fight, Romeo tries to part them, and Tybalt stabs Mercutio under Romeo's arm. Tybalt runs offstage.	
Mercutio	I am hurt.	
	A plague on both your houses! I am sped.	
	Is he gone and hath nothing?	
Benvolio	What, art thou hurt?	
Mercutio	Ay, ay, a scratch, a scratch. Marry, 'tis enough.	65
	Fetch a surgeon. *Exit Page.*	
Romeo	Courage man, the hurt cannot be much.	
Mercutio	No, 'tis not so deep as a well, nor so wide as a church door; but 'tis enough, 'twill serve. Ask for me tomorrow, and you shall find me a grave man.	70
	A plague o' both your houses! Why the devil came you between us? I was hurt under your arm.	
Romeo	I thought all for the best.	
Mercutio	Help me into some house, Benvolio,	
	Or I shall faint. A plague o' both your houses!	75
	They have made worms' meat of me.	
	I have it, and soundly too. Your houses!	
	Mercutio exits, helped by Benvolio and the servants.	
Romeo	This gentleman hath got his mortal hurt	
	In my behalf. O sweet Juliet,	
	Thy beauty hath made me effeminate	80
	And in my temper softened valour's steel.	

2 **How does Shakespeare present the character of Tybalt in *Romeo and Juliet*?**

3 **One of the themes of Romeo and Juliet is fate. How is this presented in the play?**

Globe Education Shorter Shakespeare

Series Editors: Paul Shuter, Georghia Ellinas

Contributors: Jane Sheldon, Jane Shuter, Kevin Dyke, Paul Shuter and, for the original text, Patrick Spottiswoode, Georghia Ellinas, Paul Shuter.

The text of this edition is based on the text of *Globe Education Shakespeare: Romeo and Juliet* (Hodder Education, 2011) and has been developed from the cut produced by Bill Buckhurst for the 2013 *Playing Shakespeare with Deutsche Bank* production of *Romeo and Juliet*.

This book is dedicated to Bill Buckhurst and the cast, crew and creatives of the 2013 Playing Shakespeare with Deutsche Bank production of Romeo and Juliet, who made this play live for thousands of London school students.

Playing Shakespeare with Deutsche Bank is Globe Education's flagship project for London schools, with 20,000 free tickets given to students for a full-scale Shakespeare production created specifically for young people. **www.playingshakespeare.org**

Photo credits:

All photographs are from the Shakespeare's Globe photo library. Full details of the cast and creatives of the featured productions can be found at www.shakespearesglobe.com/ShorterR&J

Andy Bradshaw, 2004 production: 18, 34, 58, 72
Manuel Harlan, spring 2009 production: 44, 56
John Haynes, summer 2009 production: 12 (top), 16, 22, 26, 32, 36, 38, 40, 48, 60, 74, 80
Ellie Kurttz, 2013 production: 6, 8, 10, 12 (bottom), 14, 20, 24, 28, 30, 42, 46, 50, 52, 54, 62, 64, 66, 68, 70, 76, 78, 82, 84, 86, 88, 90
Pete Le May: 4

John Wildgoose and Deutsche Bank, 2013 production: 52

Every effort has been made to trace all copyright holders, but if any have been inadvertently overlooked the Publishers will be pleased to make the necessary arrangements at the first opportunity.

Orders: please contact Hachette UK Distribution, Hely Hutchinson Centre, Milton Road, Didcot, Oxfordshire, OX11 7HH. Telephone: +44 (0)1235 827827. Email education@hachette.co.uk. Lines are open from 9 a.m. to 5 p.m., Monday to Friday. You can also order through our website: www.hoddereducation.co.uk.

Cover photograph Will Featherstone as Romeo and Jade Anouka as Juliet, 2013, photograph Ellie Kurttz

Typeset in ITC Century Light 10pt by DC Graphic Design Limited, Hextable Village, Kent

Printed and bound by CPI Group (UK) Ltd, Croydon, CR0 4YY

A catalogue record for this title is available from the British Library
ISBN: 978 1471 89668 2